EDITORIAL DIRECTOR   Julie A. Schumacher
SENIOR EDITOR   Terry Ofner
EDITOR   Rebecca Christian
PERMISSIONS   Laura Pieper
                          Lisa Lorimor

COVER ART   RIDING THE WIND 1997 Carey Moore

© 2000 Perfection Learning® Corporation
1000 North Second Avenue
P.O. Box 500, Logan, Iowa 51546-0500
Tel: 1-800-831-4190 • Fax: 1-800-543-2745

78851

ISBN-13: 978-0-7891-5275-6

ISBN-10: 0-7891-5275-4

21 22 23 24 PP 18 17 16 15 14

TABLE OF CONTENTS

Features of the Student Book

Introducing the Theme

Preface The Preface introduces the student to the **Essential Question** of the book. This question, together with the cluster questions and thinking skills, will guide student reading throughout the anthology. Use the Preface to set a purpose for reading.

Prologue The Prologue combines a strong visual image with a thematically relevant poem. The Prologue is designed to stimulate discussion and to set the tone for study of the anthology.

Creating Context The Creating Context section contains an essay and photo essay, as well as a concept vocabulary page. These features will create a framework for learning and provide an opportunity to assess prior knowledge.

The Selections

Clusters The anthology is divided into four **clusters** of selections. The selections offer a mixture of fiction, nonfiction, poetry, and drama.

Cluster Questions and Thinking Skills The selections in all but the last cluster are grouped around a **cluster question** and **thinking skill,** which are stated on the cluster opening page. Reading the selections in the cluster will help students answer the cluster question as well as exercise the thinking skill.

Responding to the Cluster Rather than interrupting the flow of reading with questions after every selection, *Literature & Thought* anthologies present discussion questions at the end of the cluster. Many of these discussion questions address more than one selection, giving students the opportunity to address a group of literary selections as a whole rather than as unconnected parts. These questions can also be used as prewriting prompts for the writing activity that follows the cluster questions.

Writing Activity All but the last cluster end with a writing activity that integrates the cluster question with the thinking skill.

The Final Cluster

The Final Cluster Having practiced several thinking skills and with a core of literature behind them, students should be able to approach the final cluster of selections independently.

Features of This Teacher Guide

Planning and Scheduling Options Use these strategies for planning a 4- to 6-week unit, a 1- to 2-week unit, or using the student book in conjunction with a novel.

What Do You Think? (anticipation guide) To assess your students' attitudes toward the theme of ecology, administer the anticipation guide on page 64.

Introducing the Theme These resources include strategies for teaching the Preface to set the **purpose** for reading; the Prologue for setting the **tone** of the theme study; and the Creating Context section for setting the framework, or **context**, of the unit.

Teaching the Critical Thinking Skill Each cluster in the teacher guide begins with a lesson plan and handout/overhead for modeling the cluster thinking skill.

Cluster Vocabulary Handouts and Tests Students can use the reproducible vocabulary sheet to reference challenging words in each selection and to prepare for the Cluster Vocabulary Tests.

Selection Resources Every selection in the student book is supported with the following teacher supports: selection summaries, reading hints, thinking skills, extension activities, discussion questions with suggested answers, and special focus sections that provide historical, literary, or bibliographic background on the selections.

Responding to the Cluster This resource page provides sample answers to the cluster questions.

Writing Activity Reproducible Sheet This graphic organizer integrates the writing activity and the cluster critical thinking skill.

Suggestions for Teaching the Final Cluster The final cluster provides an opportunity for students to demonstrate their mastery of the content knowledge and thinking skills. Look for the following features: a final cluster planning guide, cluster vocabulary, selection teacher support, handouts to help generate research, writing, and project ideas.

The Essay Prompt This open-book essay prompt is based on the *essential question* of the anthology. Use it as a culminating essay test. You may want to give extra credit to students who correctly use Concept Vocabulary words and words from the Cluster Vocabulary Sheets.

Sample Rubric Use or adapt the sample rubric prior to assigning, and while assessing, student writing.

Assessments

Discussing the Selection Use the discussion questions to assess student understanding of the selections.

Responding to the Cluster The questions on the Responding to the Cluster pages can be used as informal assessments of student understanding of the cluster content as well as the cluster thinking skill.

Cluster Vocabulary Tests These 10-point vocabulary tests assess student understanding of key vocabulary words.

Writing Activities Writing activities are ideal for assessing student understanding of the content and thinking skills of each cluster.

Essay Prompt Use the final essay prompt to assess student understanding of the *essential question* of the theme study.

Three Teaching Options for *What on Earth?*

4- TO 6-WEEK UNIT

Introducing the theme (1 to 2 days)

	Page Numbers In	
	Student Book	Teacher Guide

Read and discuss the following sections
- What Do You Think? (anticipation guide) 9, 64
- Preface 3. 8
- Prologue 4–5. 8
- Creating Context 9–14. 9

Teaching the first three clusters (3 to 5 days per cluster)
- Introduce and model the cluster thinking
  skill using overhead/handout 11, 23, 35
- Pass out cluster vocabulary sheet. 12, 24, 36
- Set schedule for reading selections in first three clusters
- For each selection, use appropriate discussion
  questions and extension activities
  - Cluster One 16–43. 13–18
  - Cluster Two 46–77. 25–30
  - Cluster Three 80–107. 37–44
- As a class or in small groups discuss the **Responding
  to the Cluster** questions . . . . 44, 78, 108. . . . . . . 19, 31, 45
- Introduce Writing Activity with handout . . . . 44, 78, 108. . . . . . . 20, 32, 46
- Administer Vocabulary Test 21, 33, 47

Teaching the last cluster (5 to 10 days)

The final section can be structured as a teacher-directed cluster or as independent learning.
Choose from the two models described below.

Teacher-Directed
- Pass out cluster vocabulary sheet. 51
- Set schedule for reading selections
- For each selection, use appropriate discussion
  questions and extension activities 52–57
- Administer Vocabulary Test 58
- Assign research projects. 59–60
- Administer final essay test 61

Independent Learning
Have students
- Respond to one or more of the questions or activities
  on the Responding to Cluster Four page 143
- Plan and present a lesson over one or more of the
  selections in the last cluster. 110–142
- Conduct additional research on a related topic 59–60

Three Teaching Options for *What on Earth?*

1- TO 2-WEEK UNIT

Shorten the 4- to 6-week schedule by using one or more of the following strategies.

- Assign complete clusters to literary circles. Have each group share what they learn and/or teach the cluster to their classmates.
- Assign individual selections to groups. Have each group share what they learn and/or teach the selection to the entire class.
- Choose 8–10 significant selections for study by the entire class. The following list would provide a shortened exploration of the themes in *What on Earth?*

Title	Page	Title	Page
The Growin' of Paul Bunyan	16	Heroes for the Planet: Then and Now	80
Nacho Loco	34		
Baptisms	42	David Meets Goliath at City Hall	96
A Fable for Tomorrow	46	A Young Environmentalist Speaks Out	110
When Nature Comes Too Close	59		
A Sound of Thunder	64	The Last Dog	124

USING *WHAT ON EARTH?* WITH RELATED LITERATURE

Before Reading the Related Work

- Introduce the theme and the purpose for reading using the Anticipation Guide (page 64 of this teacher guide). From *What on Earth?* use the Preface (page 3), the Prologue (pages 4–5), and Creating Context (pages 9–14).
- Have students choose one or two selections and a poem to read from each cluster. Ask students to report on their selection and how it helped them answer the cluster question.

During Reading

- Ask students to relate the readings in *What on Earth?* to themes, actions, or statements in the longer work.
- At strategic points, have students discuss how characters in the longer work would react to selections in the anthology.

After Reading

- Have students read the last cluster and respond to the cluster questions, drawing upon selections in the anthology as well as the longer work.
- Ask students to compare and contrast one or more selections in the anthology and a theme in the longer work.
- Allow students to choose a research topic from the options given in Research, Writing, and Discussion Topics (page 59) or Assessment and Project Ideas (page 60).

> **Related Longer Works**
>
> **Pilgrim at Tinker Creek** by Annie Dillard. [RL 9 IL 9 +] Paperback 5597301; Cover Craft 5597302.
>
> **Phoenix Rising** by Karen Hesse. [RL 6 IL 5–9] Paperback 4805001; Cover Craft 4805002.
>
> **A Place Called Ugly** by Avi. [RL 5.8 IL 5–9] Paperback 4646001; Cover Craft 4646002.
>
> See page 63 of this guide for descriptions of these works and more related titles.

Teaching the Preface (page 3)

How Do We Protect Our Planet?

The question above is the *essential question* that students will consider as they read the *What on Earth?* anthology. The literature, activities, and organization of the book will lead them to think critically about this question and to develop a deeper understanding of the earth and the environment.

To help them shape their answers to the broad essential question, they will read and respond to four sections, or clusters. Each cluster addresses a specific question and thinking skill.

CLUSTER ONE What Is Our Relationship with Nature? **EVALUATING**
CLUSTER TWO What Happens When Humanity and Nature Collide? **ANALYZING**
CLUSTER THREE How Can We Live in Harmony with Nature? **PROBLEM SOLVING**
CLUSTER FOUR Thinking on your own **SYNTHESIZING**

Notice that the final cluster asks students to think independently about their answer to the essential question—*How do we protect our planet?*

Discussing the Preface Review the Preface with students. Point out the essential question as well as the cluster question addressed in each cluster. You may want to revisit the essential question after students complete each cluster. The last cluster addresses the essential question directly.

Teaching the Prologue (pages 4–5)

About the Poem In his poem, "Only a Little Planet," Lawrence Collins describes the earth as small, mild, and soft. If you stop and look, he says, you'll see that we are constantly interacting with our beautiful planet.

Discussing the Poem
- Why do you think the speaker in the poem believes it is important to "stop" and "let yourself see . . ."?
- What might the speaker in the poem mean by "everything is doing things to you as you do things to everything"?
- What do the similes "like a rainbow" and "like a bubble" say about the earth?

What Do You Think? (Anticipation Guide)

Use the reproducible anticipation guide on page 64 of this teacher guide to assess your students' attitudes toward the theme of ecology. Explain that their initial ideas might change as they explore the topic more deeply. You might want to have students complete the survey again at the end of their thematic study to see how their opinions have changed. Explain that *A* stands for "agree" and *D* for "disagree."

_____ 1. Eventually humans will have to wear oxygen masks to survive the effects of air pollution.

_____ 2. After either a man-made or natural disaster occurs, the earth is often able to heal itself.

_____ 3. It is the duty of humans to protect wildlife.

_____ 4. Since extinction is a natural process, it doesn't matter if humans cause the extinction of a certain species.

_____ 5. Overpopulation is a crucial problem throughout the world.

_____ 6. Most Americans are not willing to be inconvenienced to help solve an environmental issue.

_____ 7. Hunting is murder and should be banned.

_____ 8. In the last few years, the weather has gotten much worse due to man-made causes.

Teaching the Creating Context Section (pages 9–14)

Use these Creating Context features to activate students' prior knowledge and build background about ecology and environmental issues.

Butterfly or Asteroid? (pages 9–10)

The essay describes two stories told by scientists who study the history of life on earth. According to "chaos theory," something as slight as the beat of a butterfly's wings can cause major changes in the weather. And according to another theory, a huge asteroid that crashed into the earth caused the extinction of the dinosaurs. Humans are more like the butterfly, the essay concludes, because our smallest actions can have great consequences.

Discussing the Essay

- The essay asks whether we—the humans on earth—are more like a butterfly or a giant asteroid. What is implied by each of these similes?
- Which environmental dangers do you think would be most difficult to combat: those that are as powerful as a giant asteroid or those that are caused by the beat of a butterfly's wing?
- What do students think nature photographer Mark Carwardine means when he says, "The darker it gets, the faster we're driving"?

Thinking Naturally (pages 11–13)

About the Images and Quotes This collage features the photos and comments of eight environmentalists.

- Are there any differing points of view that you believe should be added to this collage? If so, what are they?
- If you could choose one of the ecologists pictured as your companion on a hike, who would it be and why?

Concept Vocabulary (page 14)

The terms on these pages are important to understanding the selections on ecology.

Discussing Concept Vocabulary

- Discuss terms that may be new to students.
- Have students add new concept words as they read the anthology.

CLUSTER ONE

Evaluating

I. Present this definition to students.

Evaluation is the process of making a judgment based on standards or criteria.

II. Discuss with students how they already use evaluation by sharing the situations below.

You use evaluation when you

- choose which movie you want to see
- decide whether a move is legal according to the rules of a game
- judge whether a punishment is fair
- decide whether you want to be friends with someone

III. Explain to students that as a class they will be surveying their attitudes about nature.

A. Use the reproducible "Nature and Us: A Class Survey" on the next page as an overhead transparency or blackline master.

B. Ask students to evaluate their own attitudes toward nature by marking "agree" or "disagree" by each numbered statement. Then ask them to score their statements using the guideline given to determine whether they are avidly interested in nature, mildly interested in nature, or indifferent to nature. They may also want to compile the results of their individual survey in order to evaluate their attitudes toward nature as a class.

C. Finally, ask students if they think the survey provides a fair and accurate measure of attitudes toward nature. If not, ask them to come up with questions of their own.

Nature and Us: A Class Survey

Cluster Question: What Is Our relationship With Nature?

Evaluating is the process of making a judgment based on standards or criteria. Indicate whether you agree or disagree with the statements below by filling in the blank with *A* for "agree" and *D* for "disagree."

Agree/Disagree

_____ 1. I like to spend as much time outdoors as possible.

_____ 2. I like to go camping.

_____ 3. If given a choice, I prefer being inside to being outside.

_____ 4. I associate the outdoors with discomfort: bugs, dirt, unpredictable weather.

_____ 5. There are several outdoor activities—fishing, water-skiing, hiking, or others—that I enjoy.

_____ 6. I help my family and/or school in their recycling efforts.

_____ 7. I enjoy identifying species of plants and animals.

_____ 8. I am knowledgeable and concerned about environmental issues such as pollution and global warming.

Scoring: Give yourself one point each for answering "agree" to numbers 1, 2, 5, 6, 7, and 8.
Give yourself ten points each for answering "agree" to numbers 3 and 4.

Use the following score chart to rank your attitude toward nature:

Score Chart	
If you scored between:	You are
6–8	avidly interested in nature.
9–15	moderately interested in nature.
16–25	indifferent to nature.

Now evaluate this survey. Do you think it fairly and accurately measured your attitude toward nature? If not, come up with some survey statements of your own.

Cluster One Vocabulary

Watch for the following words as you read the selections in Cluster One. Record your own vocabulary words and definitions on the blank lines.

The Growin' of Paul Bunyan pages 16–23

philosophical difference conflict in belief; disagreement
rankles annoys; irritates
wrought up excited; agitated

_____

_____

_____

_____

The Wisdomkeepers pages 24–27

assemblage collection; assortment
exploit abuse; take advantage of
precarious risky; unstable
replica copy; duplicate
shrouded hidden; obscured
sovereignty power; leadership
steward caretaker; custodian

_____

_____

_____

_____

For Richard Chase page 28

coves nooks; caves
hover float; flutter

_____

_____

_____

_____

Is Humanity a Special Threat? pages 29–33

degradation a downgrading; a reduction in quality
expended used up; consumed
fervor craze; overwhelming enthusiasm
negligence carelessness; neglect
pristine clean; unsullied
regenerative healing; restoring
residue remains; remnant

_____

_____

_____

_____

Nacho Loco pages 34–41

barbarian savage; brute
ricocheted rebounded; bounced
scuttled scurried; moved like a crab

_____

_____

_____

_____

Baptisms pages 42–43

dominion control; supremacy
residing living; dwelling

_____

_____

_____

_____

The Growin' of Paul Bunyan by William J. Brooke, pages 16–23 Folk Tale

Summary

The gigantic Paul Bunyan likes to cut down trees, especially when he's annoyed by something, such as a moose stuck between his toes. When Bunyan crosses paths with Johnny Appleseed—a man who plants apple trees and magically hastens their growth—Bunyan cuts down trees faster than Appleseed can grow them. Through gentle persuasion, Appleseed changes the huge logger's attitude.

Reading Hint	Thinking Skill	Extension
Point out that this tale is written in dialect (a variation from standard language that is spoken by a particular group).	Ask students to *evaluate* the method Johnny Appleseed uses to change Paul Bunyan's attitude toward trees.	**Applying Strategy:** Ask students to think of ways that Appleseed's strategy could be applied to other problems. For example, how might students help others take an interest in the condition of a park, school, or other community area?

Vocabulary

philosophical difference conflict in belief; disagreement

rankles annoys; irritates

wrought up excited; agitated

Discussing the Folk Tale

1. What do Paul Bunyan and Johnny Appleseed have in common? (Recall) *Paul Bunyan comments that they both like trees. Also, each man wanders the land alone, doing "what he does."*

2. What is their philosophical difference? (Recall) *Johnny Appleseed likes trees vertical—upright and alive. Paul Bunyan likes trees horizontal—cut and available for use.*

3. What is the meaning of the title of the story? (Analysis) *Answers may vary. Some students may say that "growin'" refers to the trees that Paul Bunyan finally grew. Others may point out that Bunyan himself grew by learning how to grow trees.*

4. How does this story describe Paul Bunyan's character? (Analysis) *Answers may vary. Bunyan seems none too bright. He is slow to understand Johnny Appleseed's attitude and is persistent about doing what he does—cutting down trees. But he is also basically cordial, even in a philosophical disagreement. Finally, Bunyan is able to learn from experience and is open to change.*

Special Focus: Folk Tales, Tall Tales, and Legends

Traditionally, folk tales are imaginative, entertaining stories, passed down orally. Tall tales—often considered a type of folk tale—are especially fanciful stories that feature heroic figures who may or may not have actually lived. Paul Bunyan became a hero of many tall tales, even though his origins were not in folklore. The giant lumberjack was actually created in the early part of the 20th century as a character in a lumber company advertisement.

Legends are stories with some foundation in truth. American frontier legends include such heroes as Daniel Boone, Davy Crockett, and Calamity Jane. John Chapman was an actual person who traveled the country planting apple trees, which earned him the nickname "Johnny Appleseed." So this story brings together an imaginary hero of tall tales and a legend based on a real man. Use the following questions to prompt discussion.

- What modern person might you use as a model for a legend about ecology?
- What fictional hero could you invent to champion the cause of nature?

The Wisdomkeepers by Harvey Arden and Steve Wall, pages 24–27   Interview

Summary

Oren Lyons, a spokesman for the Onondaga tribe, describes Native American attitudes toward the environment. He discusses natural law, man's law, common sense toward the environment, and human responsibility for the world and generations to come. He says that the red and white cultures are parallel and equal but that trying to straddle them can be dangerous.

Reading Hint	Thinking Skill	Extension
Point out that the interviewers describe the opening scene, but after the subhead "The Natural Law," the words are those of Oren Lyons.	Ask students to *evaluate* why Oren Lyons prefers not to use telephones or electricity.	**Law vs. Law:** Have students come up with their own definitions of man's law and natural law.

Vocabulary

assemblage collection; assortment

exploit abuse; take advantage of

precarious risky; unstable

replica copy; duplicate

shrouded hidden; obscured

sovereignty power; leadership

steward caretaker; custodian

Discussing the Interview

1. What are the two kinds of laws discussed in this interview? (Recall) *Oren Lyons says that the law made by government is man's law; the law made by the creator is natural law, which is greater than man's law.*

2. According to Lyons, what kind of law is the most dangerous to break? (Recall) *If you break man's law, you may be fined or sent to jail, or you may escape punishment. However, there's no escaping the consequences of breaking natural law—"you're going to get hit and get hit hard," according to Lyons.*

3. Evaluate Lyon's statement that "all life is equal." (Analysis) *Answers may vary. In some ways, insects, for example, must be considered as important as other life forms in order to maintain a natural ecological balance. On the other hand, we do not generally value the lives of plants, insects, or animals above those of humans.*

4. What does it mean to be a steward of the earth? (Analysis) *Answers may vary. A steward is one who manages property or affairs for the owner. The implication is that human beings are managing the earth and that we have a responsibility to do a good job.*

Special Focus: Dominion or Equality?

Like Oren Lyons, some people believe all life is equal. Others believe that people should have dominion over animals and plants. Prompt discussion with students with the following questions.

- Should people take dominion over animals? Explain.
- Do plants have rights? Why or why not?
- Even if they want to, is it possible for people to take dominion over nature? Explain.

For Richard Chase by Jim Wayne Miller, page 28   Poem

Summary

The poem describes an old storyteller who visits a California high school classroom. As he speaks, the craggy storyteller shows the students a seashell. However, the student who listens to the seashell "hears" the freeway instead of the sounds of nature.

Reading Hint	Thinking Skill	Extension
Explain that poets sometimes dedicate their work to a person. It is not clear who Richard Chase is—he might be the storyteller in the poem; he may be someone else—a fellow poet, for example.	Ask students to *evaluate* how and why the author uses images from nature to describe the mountain man.	**Using Nature's Images:** Ask students to write their own descriptions of another person, using images from nature or the city to develop a vivid image.

Vocabulary

coves nooks; caves

hover float; flutter

Discussing the Poem

1. What happens at the beginning of the poem? (Recall) *An "old tale-teller from the mountains" visits a high school classroom in California.*

2. How does the author support his statement that the mountain man "is himself a mountain"? (Recall) *The poet compares the old man's face to coves and hollows, his shoulders to ridges, his eyes to hawks' eyes. The old man's stories pour forth like mountain streams; his silences are like rock.*

3. What impression do you get of the storyteller's speaking style? (Analysis) *Answers may vary. His speech is described as trickling off his tongue, falling, flowing, tumbling— giving an impression of fluent and perhaps exciting speech.*

4. What is the significance of the last line? (Analysis) *Answers will vary. The last line reveals the vast, and possibly insurmountable, differences between the culture of the old man from the mountains and the students from the city.*

Special Focus: City vs. Country Life

This poem explores the relationship of city life and country life through the use of simile and metaphor. The storyteller arrives "looking like all outdoors," and "He himself is a mountain." The tension between the country and the city also comes through when the student thinks the inside of the shell sounds like a freeway. Ask students to explore their own attitudes by inventing similes and metaphors that relate themselves to either the city and/or the country.

Discuss the following.

- If the storyteller is like a mountain, what is the student in the poem like?

- If the freeway is like an ocean, what other similes or metaphors could you use to liken human-made objects to natural ones?

- What simile or metaphor could you use to illustrate your own relationship to either the country or the city?

Is Humanity a Special Threat? by Gregg Easterbrook, pages 29–33   Essay

Summary

Three years after the *Exxon Valdez* oil spill in Alaska's Prince William Sound, Gregg Easterbrook returns to the site, traveling on a research vessel under the sponsorship of the National Oceanographic and Atmospheric Administration. Easterbrook observes that the effects of the spill are no longer visible and that the clean-up efforts appear to have done more damage than the spill itself.

Reading Hint	Thinking Skill	Extension
Point out that the oil spill discussed in the article occurred in 1989; this selection was published six years later, in 1995.	*Evaluate* the evidence that Easterbrook presents for making no clean-up efforts after a spill.	**Other Points of View:** Ask your class how Oren Lyons in "Wisdomkeepers" would respond to this essay.

Vocabulary

degradation a downgrading; a reduction in quality

expended used up; consumed

fervor craze; overwhelming enthusiasm

negligence carelessness; neglect

pristine clean; unsullied

regenerative healing; restoring

residue remains; remnant

Discussing the Essay

1. What event started the controversy that Easterbrook writes about? (Recall) *In March 1989, the tanker* Exxon Valdez *struck a reef in Alaska's Prince William Sound and spilled 11 million gallons of crude oil.*

2. What does the author say was responsible for panic over the oil spill? (Recall) *Easterbrook says that pictures of oil fouling the wilderness taken by television and news-magazine cameras aroused public and governmental hysteria.*

3. Evaluate Easterbrook's statement that "overall nature shrugged off the *Exxon Valdez* 'disaster' as if shooing away a mosquito." (Analysis) *Answers may vary. The author gives evidence of considerable recovery, but does mention lasting harm to wildlife, including birds and killer whales. Some students may agree with Easterbrook; others may feel that he is minimizing the damage.*

4. What is your reaction to making no clean-up efforts should another oil spill occur? (Analysis) *Answers may vary, but most students will probably agree that to do nothing seems extreme and that each situation should be analyzed by experts, keeping the outcome of the* Exxon Valdez *oil spill in mind.*

Special Focus: Writing with an Agenda

Easterbrook's essay is an example of writing with an agenda. He uses the *Exxon Valdez* example to prove his overall theory that many environmental activists become too extreme with their solutions after a man-made problem occurs. He maintains that earth is generally able to heal itself. As in any form of persuasive writing, he tries to make the reader agree with his opinion. A good persuasive writer should avoid weaknesses such as either-or thinking (oversimplifying an argument into just two sides) and circular reasoning (stating a point as a given when it really needs to be demonstrated).

Use the following to prompt discussion.

• What are the essay's strengths?

• Do you see any evidence of the weaknesses described above? Give examples.

• Do you agree with Easterbrook, disagree, or need to know more about the issue before forming an opinion? Why?

Nacho Loco by Gary Soto, pages 34–41   Short Story

Summary

Ignacio "Nacho" Carrillo's teacher suggests things her students can do to help save the earth, including recycling, planting trees, and eating a vegetarian diet. When Nacho decides to become a vegetarian, he faces parental disapproval and constant temptation.

Reading Hint	Thinking Skill	Extension
Call attention to the Spanish terms used but not defined in the text. Have students use context clues before looking at the footnote translations.	*Evaluate* the reasons Nacho gives for being a vegetarian. Are they solid?	**Topic for Debate:** Divide your class into teams to debate the statement: "For the welfare of your body and the planet, you should not eat meat."

Vocabulary

barbarian savage; brute

ricocheted rebounded; bounced

scuttled scurried; moved like a crab

Discussing the Short Story

1. Why do Nacho and his brother Felipe become vegetarians? (Recall) *Nacho tries to become a vegetarian because his teacher tells him it is one way to save the planet. Felipe became a vegetarian only because a girlfriend talked him into it.*

2. What makes it difficult for Nacho to be a vegetarian? (Recall) *He tends to forget his resolve, and he is surrounded by temptations—forbidden foods, ads for burgers, and reminders of pizzas. In addition, his brother gets a new girlfriend and gives up vegetarianism.*

3. Do you think that Nacho will remain a vegetarian? Explain. (Analysis) *Answers will vary. Some students may say that he has successfully resisted temptation; others may believe that the temptations will finally get to him.*

4. Do you think vegetarians are friendlier to the earth than meat eaters? (Analysis) *Answers will vary.*

Special Focus: Vegetarianism

People who are vegetarians eat only plant products, such as grains, beans, vegetables, and fruits. They avoid eating animal flesh, including red meat, poultry, and fish. Some vegetarians also avoid dairy products.

People may be vegetarians because of their religious or cultural beliefs. For example, some Indian and Asian religions regard the eating of animals as a violation of the ethical principle of nonviolence. Other people refuse to eat meat because they find the methods of raising animals offensive or because they believe that vegetables and fruits provide a healthier diet than meat. Still others become vegetarians for ecological reasons, since less land and fewer resources are required to grow vegetables and grain than to raise livestock.

Prompt discussion with these questions.

- Is there an ethical difference between eating meat from a cellophane wrapped package in a grocery store and eating game you have hunted yourself?
- Can one person's sacrifice—whether the issue is meat-eating or recycling—make a difference? Explain.

Baptisms by Joseph Bruchac, pages 42–43 — Poem

Summary

This poem describes a shift in the names of people from Native American, nature-related words to the craft-related words of European immigrants. The new people changed the names of the earlier people and also of the places. But there are whispers that the change continues and a new set of names may possibly be given.

Reading Hint	Thinking Skill	Extension
Point out that in its more general use, a *baptism* is any ceremony by which one is purified, initiated into a group, and/or given a name.	Ask students what they think the speaker in the poem means by "things have not ended as they should."	**Names with Meaning:** Ask your students to discuss what each group of names means and why they think each group used certain kinds of names. They might also speculate on what kinds of names might be used for future generations.

Vocabulary

dominion control; supremacy

residing living; dwelling

Discussing the Poem

1. According to the poem, why did the first people and the new ones give themselves different kinds of names? (Recall) *The first people believed that they became what they were named. The new ones named themselves for skills that gave them control over the land.*

2. Why did the new ones also change the names of the first people? (Recall) *They gave them different names and "waited for them to change" so that they would become more European.*

3. What is the significance of the changes in place names? (Analysis) *The fourth stanza implies that the Native American lands have been overrun by the new names and by places such as Breeder Reactor, Missile Range, etc. The last line "things have not ended as they should" implies that something is wrong with this change or that the change isn't over yet.*

4. What is implied by the last stanza? (Analysis) *Answers may vary. The last stanza implies that change is again about to happen, but that readers don't yet know what kind of change. The line "the Sun is rising, breathing again / names which we have not yet heard" may indicate that the new names will reveal a return to nature.*

Special Focus: The Power of Names

"Baptisms" implies that the names given to people and places might have a very real effect on them. In folktales and myths from around the world, names are said to have magical power. Secret names, known only to their owners, are important in such stories, and knowing a person's secret name could give one power over that person.

To many Native American cultures, the naming of a child was an important ceremony. Some believed that a person could become sick if his or her name didn't fit well. Then the old name would be "washed off" and a new one given. Discuss the following with students.

- Is there a story behind your name, either first or last?
- If you had to change your name, what would you change it to?
- If people invented their names from occupations in high technology, what might some of those names be?

What Is Our Relationship with Nature?

Thinking Skill: EVALUATING

1. Consider each character in this cluster, and **evaluate** his or her relationship with nature. Then place them on a continuum chart such as the one below. Be prepared to explain your placement. *Answers will vary. Students may not put any characters at the destroyer end of the continuum. They might consider the following: Johnny Appleseed makes plants and nurtures trees, and teaches Paul Bunyan to do the same. Paul Bunyan destroyed trees at one time but changes his attitude. Oren Lyons discusses respect for all life and regards humans as stewards of nature. Confused as he is, Ignacio Carrillo still makes an effort to protect nature.*

2. Characters in "The Growin' of Paul Bunyan" speak in dialect. Some readers find this amusing; others are irritated by it. Did the dialect add to or subtract from your enjoyment of the story? Be prepared to explain your answer. *Answers will vary. Dialect makes a story seem as if it is being spoken. Students may feel that the dialect adds enjoyment to the piece. Others may find the dialect distracting or offensive—as though the author is poking fun.*

3. How do you think a person who relies on the lumber industry for a living would respond to "The Growin' of Paul Bunyan"? *The lumber industry might find much to dislike here—especially since Paul Bunyan was once used as a symbol of the perfect lumberjack. Paul Bunyan in this story hacks down trees for fun but learns about growing trees instead and stops. Today's lumber industry does replant trees in areas it has clear-cut, but the idea that Bunyan has stopped cutting altogether surely doesn't fit with their business plans.*

4. How would the following people respond to the essay "Is Humanity a Special Threat?": the president of Exxon, a member of an environmental group such as Greenpeace, and Oren Lyons in "Wisdomkeepers"? *Answers will vary. For example, the president of Exxon might object. The company spent money in highly publicized efforts to clean up their oil spill, and the article questions the effectiveness of their methods. Still, Exxon might like the idea that nothing should be done if such a spill occurs again. A member of an environmental group would likely question the author's ideas, pointing out that a lack of visible damage at a spill site doesn't mean damage hasn't occurred. Oren Lyons might think that such an insult to the earth could not be repaired.*

5. In the poem "Baptisms," the speaker says that some seek "dominion over rock and stream, ownership of forest and plain." How does an attitude of "dominion" or "ownership" affect how we manage our natural resources, in both good and bad ways? *Answers will vary. Some people believe that the natural world is here for human use—an owner can do whatever he or she wants with property. For others, dominion implies stewardship. This means that we have the responsibility to be good caretakers—for our own sake as well as that of the earth.*

6. Evaluate your relationship with nature; then place yourself on the continuum chart from question one and explain your placement. *Answers will vary.*

Writing Activity: Position Paper

The handout on the next page provides a graphic organizer to help students with the writing activity. You may wish to use the Writing Activity Handout as an assessment. See also page 62 for a sample rubric to use with student essays and projects.

Writing Activity: Position Paper

Pick one of the following quotations and write a position paper on why you agree or disagree with it. Use the steps below to prepare your thoughts.

> *". . . there's nobody bigger than a man who learns to grow."*
>   from "The Growin' of Paul Bunyan"
>
> *"You don't fool around with Natural law and get away with it."*
>   from "Wisdomkeepers"
>
> *". . . the smartest thing they could have done after the [Exxon Valdez oil] spill is not one single thing."*
>   from "Is Humanity A Special Threat?"

I.   Decide which quotation you wish to write about.

II.   Do you agree or disagree with the quotation? _____

III. Write down three to five reasons for your position.

      A. _____

      B. _____

      C. _____

      D. _____

      E. _____

IV.   Use the strongest three reasons in your paper. Support your reasoning with details: examples, facts, explanations.

A position paper
- begins with a statement of the writer's opinion.
- uses examples to support the opinion.
- presents information clearly and logically.
- concludes by restating the writer's opinion.

Cluster One Vocabulary Test

Concept Vocabulary Words

Choose the meaning of the bold word in each passage.

1. He'd been so **wrought up**, he'd cleared all the way to the southern edge o' the woods without noticin'. *(The Growin' of Paul Bunyan, p. 18)*

   Ⓐ sick   Ⓒ excited
   Ⓑ tired   Ⓓ bored

2. Now that **rankles** Paul. When he beats somebody fair an' square, he expects that someone to admit it like a man. *(The Growin' of Paul Bunyan, p. 21)*

   Ⓐ stops   Ⓒ pleases
   Ⓑ annoys   Ⓓ hurts

3. This is a replica of the Two Row Wampum, the basis of our **sovereignty**. *(The Wisdomkeepers, p. 27)*

   Ⓐ family   Ⓒ history
   Ⓑ power   Ⓓ belief

4. That's a very **precarious** position to be in. *(The Wisdomkeepers, p. 27)*

   Ⓐ silly   Ⓒ high
   Ⓑ risky   Ⓓ advantageous

5. He himself is a mountain: his face has the lay of **coves** and hollows. *(For Richard Chase, p. 28)*

   Ⓐ nooks   Ⓒ ruts
   Ⓑ peaks   Ⓓ wrinkles

6. Both the **negligence** that caused the spill and arrogance of Exxon executives . . . represented corporate unaccountability at its most offensive. *(Is Humanity a Special Threat? p. 29)*

   Ⓐ enthusiasm   Ⓒ crimes
   Ⓑ carelessness Ⓓ accident

7. . . . this huge sum of money was **expended** in an enterprise that probably was unneeded and may have done more harm than good. *(Is Humanity a Special Threat? p. 32)*

   Ⓐ budgeted   Ⓒ earned
   Ⓑ borrowed   Ⓓ used up

8. Juan's cellophane **scuttled** in a light breeze, and Nacho picked it up. *(Nacho Loco, p. 37)*

   Ⓐ scurried   Ⓒ dropped
   Ⓑ sank   Ⓓ vibrated

9. But each time he missed, or the ball **ricocheted** away from him . . .*(Nacho Loco, p. 39)*

   Ⓐ rebounded   Ⓒ flew
   Ⓑ dribbled   Ⓓ got

10. . . . great-grandfathers seeking hard **dominion** over rock and stream . . . *(Baptisms, p. 42)*

    Ⓐ control   Ⓒ bridges
    Ⓑ passage   Ⓓ lessons

CLUSTER TWO

Analyzing

I. Present this definition to students.

In **analyzing** you break down a topic or subject into parts so that it is easier to understand.

II. Discuss with students how they already use analysis by sharing the situations below.

You use analysis when

- you study the good moves of an outstanding athlete.
- you pick out a new hair style or go shopping for new clothes.
- you learn the rules for a new game or learn how to use new software.

Have students suggest other situations where analysis would be used.

III. Explain to students that on the reproducible assignment, they will read synopses about situations in which humans and nature collide. Use the following steps to analyze the situations.

A. Use the reproducible "Analyzing Potential Problems" on the next page as an overhead transparency or blackline master.

B. Show how a reader analyzed the first situation by listing potential problems that could result from it.

C. Ask students to analyze the remaining situations.

Possible answers:
- *U.S. oil companies—could pollute the area and destroy habitat for people, plants, and animals.*
- *Real estate developers—could destroy habitat for local plant and animal life; deprive nature lovers of a place to go; change the drainage patterns of land.*
- *Group of hunters—their actions could have long-term effects on history.*

D. Instruct students to use the space provided to enter and analyze a situation with which they are familiar.

Analyzing Potential Problems

Cluster Question: What Happens When Humanity and Nature Collide?

Definition: In analyzing you break down a topic or subject into parts so that it is easier to understand.

Directions: Below are several situations involving humans and elements of nature. Read the situations, and then analyze what problems might develop. The first one has been done for you.

Situation	Potential problems
A type of insect is destroying thousands of acres of crops. Humans develop a pesticide that kills the harmful insects.	• The pesticide could kill helpful insects and harm wildlife. • Other plants could be affected if the insects that pollinate them are killed. • Extermination of the harmful insects could cause starvation of species that feed upon them. • The pesticide could be harmful to humans.
U.S. oil companies begin operations in the rain forests of South America.	
Real estate developers clear wooded areas for housing developments.	
Hunters travel back in time to hunt and kill dinosaurs.	
Your situation:	

Cluster Two Vocabulary

Watch for the following words as you read the selections in Cluster Two. Record your own vocabulary words and definitions on the blank lines.

A Fable for Tomorrow
from *Silent Spring* pages 46–49

blight plague; misfortune
counterparts equivalents; others that are very similar
maladies illnesses; ailments
moribund wasting away; dying
specter spirit; ghost

_____

_____

_____

Battle for the Rain Forest pages 50–55

elite privileged; wealthy
eradication elimination; destruction
impede block; prevent
toxic harmful; deadly

_____

_____

_____

All Revved Up About an Even Bigger
Vehicle pages 56–58

coveted desired; envied
maneuver move skillfully; manipulate
patrons customers
teeming overflowing; full of

_____

_____

_____

When Nature Comes Too Close
pages 59–63

acute severe; major
constitutes makes up; amounts to
contiguous connected; joined
dearth lack; scarcity
indicative suggestive; representative
prohibitive restrictive; constraining
proliferation rapid growth; increase
wilier trickier; more clever

_____

_____

_____

A Sound of Thunder pages 64–76

aurora light; glow
correlate bring together; match
expendable replaceable; dispensable
mooring support; anchor
paradox contradiction; inconsistency
resilient flexible; springy
subliminal below conscious awareness
undulate rise and fall; ripple

_____

_____

_____

And They Lived Happily Ever After for a
While page 77

_____

_____

_____

A Fable for Tomorrow by Rachel Carson, pages 46–49   Essay
from *Silent Spring*

Summary

Carson describes a picturesque town and the surrounding countryside, both teeming with life. Then comes a strange blight that brings illness and even death to humans, plants, and wildlife in the area. Carson indicates that the cause of the blight is a white powder (probably a lethal chemical such as DDT) developed by humans for human use.

Reading Hint	Thinking Skill	Extension
Point out to students that the author of this selection, Rachel Carson, is considered a pioneer of the environmental movement.	Ask students to *analyze* how this piece may have contributed to Carson's launching of the environmental movement.	Have students debate the following statement: "Chemically derived pesticides that are harmful to humans should be banned." Have students consider such factors as economic impact and available alternatives in their arguments.

Vocabulary

blight plague; misfortune

counterparts equivalents; others that are very similar

maladies illnesses; ailments

moribund wasting away; dying

specter spirit; ghost

Discussing the Essay

1. Why might Carson have placed the setting for her fable in "the heart of America"? (Analysis) *Answers will vary. Students will probably say that Carson was making the point that such a disaster can happen anywhere.*

2. Why does one year bring a "spring without voices"? (Recall) *Much of the wildlife, including the song birds, is stricken by a strange blight.*

3. What do you think the white powder that "had fallen like snow" is? (Analysis) *Answers will vary. Students will probably suggest that the white powder is some sort of human-made chemical, such as a pesticide, herbicide, or fertilizer, meant to control or change the environment.*

Literary Focus: Fable

Tell students that a fable is a story (usually for children) that teaches a lesson. Use the following questions to discuss this selection.

- Why might this essay be called "A Fable for Tomorrow"? *Carson's lesson is a warning for the future about the repercussions of using chemical pesticides.*

- Rachel Carson was a marine biologist. Why do you think she chose to present this message as a fable rather than as a structured scientific essay? *Carson may be trying to make the point that her message is a very basic one: When nature is modified, disaster can result. If she had presented information in a scientific format, it may not have touched the hearts of as many people.*

- Has Carson's prophesy come true? *Answers will vary. Encourage students to use examples from the first cluster, such as the Exxon Valdez oil spill, to support their opinions.*

Battle for the Rain Forest by Joe Kane, pages 50–55

Article

Summary

Indigenous peoples of South America have begun to fight back against United States oil companies and their own governments. The tribes claim that the oil companies are polluting their lands, but the companies maintain that they have broken no laws. Meanwhile, the impoverished governments, who desperately need the revenue from the oil, offer little protection to the native people.

Reading Hint	Thinking Skill	Extension
Instruct students to read this article objectively, staying open to the arguments on both sides of the conflict.	Have students choose several statements made by the oil companies and *analyze* them as to their accuracy and/or validity.	**David vs. Goliath Stories:** Tell students that the conflict described in this selection could be called a "David and Goliath" conflict. One side of such a battle is typically weak while the other is overpoweringly strong. Have students think of other David and Goliath conflicts with which they're familiar. In each case, which side won? Which side do they think will win this fight? Why?

Vocabulary

elite privileged; wealthy

eradication elimination; destruction

impede block; prevent

toxic harmful; deadly

Discussing the Article

1. Why are some of the tribal peoples of South America upset with United States oil companies? (Recall) *They claim that the companies are destroying their habitat and poisoning their homelands with toxic wastes.*

2. What are some of the steps the tribes have taken in their fight against the oil companies? (Recall) *They have taken oil workers as prisoners, burned an oil well, destroyed a helicopter landing pad, threatened mass suicide, and filed a lawsuit.*

3. Why can't the native peoples get help from their governments? (Recall) *No laws to protect them or give them rights to the oil exist; the impoverished governments need the revenue from the oil, so they are reluctant to confront the companies.*

4. Do you think that payments such as the one made to the Secoya people by the oil companies are fair to the tribe? (Analysis) *Answers will vary. Some students are almost certain to point out that the oil companies*

are taking advantage of the tribes by paying them what amounts to a pittance. Others will argue that if the Secoya are satisfied with the bargain, the agreement is fair.

Special Focus: The Rain Forest

This selection brings up many issues: progress vs. an ancient lifestyle; a country's economic needs vs. the preferred lifestyle of a minority; the habits and desires of a rich nation vs. basic human rights. Use the following questions to discuss these issues with your students.

- Is it inevitable that all societies will change as a result of progress? Why or why not?
- Should the natural resources of any piece of land be controlled by the people who live there, the government of the country, or the companies that develop the land?
- Should American environmental and human-rights standards apply to U.S. companies operating overseas? Why?
- Do you think Americans would be willing to use fewer of the resources gleaned from the rain forests in order to save the forests? Why or why not?

All Revved Up About an Even Bigger Vehicle
Humor Column

by Dave Barry, pages 56–58

Summary

What America needs, according to humorist and satirist Dave Barry, is an even bigger sports utility vehicle. Barry goes on to comment on the advertised benefits versus the realities of owning such a vehicle. He concludes that, due to the consumer habits of Americans, even larger vehicles are on the way.

Reading Hint	Thinking Skill	Extension
Point out to students that Barry is fond of using *hyperbole*—extreme exaggeration—to make a point or to evoke humor.	Have students *analyze* the reasoning behind Barry's statement ". . . Cars will keep getting bigger."	**Humor with a Purpose:** Tell students that most humor has an underlying purpose. Ask students to discuss what the author's purposes were in writing this column. Did he make his point effectively? Why or why not?

Vocabulary

coveted desired; envied

maneuver move skillfully; manipulate

patrons customers

teeming overflowing; full of

Discussing the Humor Column

1. According to the author, why don't owners of sports utility vehicles drive them off-road, as they were designed to be driven? (Recall) *SUV owners have paid upward of $40,000 for their vehicles and don't want to risk damaging them.*

2. What does Barry say are the advantages and disadvantages of SUVs? (Recall) *Advantages include safety (at least for the SUV driver) and the popularity of having the Least Sane Motor Vehicles, as Barry satirically points out. Disadvantages are having to maneuver SUVs into parking spaces and being unable to see smaller cars.*

3. Why do you think SUVs are so popular? (Analysis) *Answers may vary. Students may suggest that SUVs have become status symbols.*

Literary Focus: Irony

Tell students that *irony* occurs when appearances are at odds with reality. Perhaps the most common type of irony is *verbal irony,* in which people say the opposite of what they mean. A good example of Barry's use of verbal irony is his opening line, "If there's one thing this nation needs, it's bigger cars."

In *situational irony,* events turn out differently than expected. The fact that SUVs are designed and advertised for off-road use but are seldom used that way is an example of situational irony. Use the following to discuss the use of irony in this selection.

- What are some examples of verbal irony in Barry's column? In each instance, how does Barry say the opposite of what he means?
- Find and explain examples of situational irony in the selection.
- Have students look for examples of ironic situations in previous selections in this book. *For example, in "For Richard Chase," the student who holds a shell to his ear hears the freeway instead of the ocean.*

When Nature Comes Too Close   by Anthony Brandt, pages 59–63   Article

Summary

This article discusses the growing nationwide problem of wildlife invading populated areas. Among the reasons given are human and animal population growth, changes in hunting laws, and scarcity of natural predators.

Reading Hint	Thinking Skill	Extension
Point out that although the selection opens with several paragraphs about North Haven, New York, it moves on to examine the problem of wildlife in the suburbs nationally.	Instruct students to *analyze* why the author takes the "I" and "we" approach.	Lead students in a discussion of which has the stronger right to a piece of land: the wildlife that inhabits it or the people who want to develop it.

Vocabulary

acute severe; major

constitutes makes up; amounts to

contiguous connected; joined

dearth lack; scarcity

indicative suggestive; representative

prohibitive restrictive; constraining

proliferation rapid growth; increase

wilier trickier; more clever

Discussing the Article

1. What is causing the "overlap" of people and animals described in this article? (Recall) *Some causes mentioned are hunting restrictions, human and animal population growth, lack of natural predators for many species, and human desire to conserve and observe wildlife.*

2. What are some of the problems caused by "backyard wildlife"? (Recall) *The animals cause damage to forests, to habitats of smaller animals, and to gardens. They can carry rabies and ticks with Lyme disease, cause car accidents, and kill livestock and pets.*

3. What are some possible remedies? (Recall) *The article mentions bounties, poisoning, hunting, trapping, large-scale slaughter, contraception, changing animal behavior, and moving animals to other locations. Students may have other ideas.*

4. Sum up the basic conflict presented in this article. (Analysis) *Answers will vary. Students might describe the problems in terms of both human and animal population explosions, people taking over animal habitats, or insufficient harvesting of animals.*

Special Focus: Expository Essay

Explain that this article is an *expository essay*, a type of writing designed to inform the reader. The introduction catches the reader's attention and contains a *thesis*, or belief statement, by the author. The body of the essay supports the thesis with facts, examples, or other information. The conclusion states the implications of the thesis and usually ends with a memorable statement. Further explore this type of essay by using the following questions.

- What is the thesis of "When Nature Comes Too Close"?
- Does the author provide enough facts and examples to support the thesis?
- Does the author offer a workable solution to the problem?
- Does he explore possible solutions?
- What additional visual aids—such as tables, charts, graphs, maps, illustrations, photographs, or timelines—would you use to make the information more clear?

A Sound of Thunder by Ray Bradbury, pages 64–76 Short Story

Summary

A group of hunters travels back in time to hunt dinosaurs. They bag their *Tyrannosaurus rex*, but one man stumbles off the designated path, stepping on a butterfly and changing the course of history.

Reading Hint	Thinking Skill	Extension
The dramatic tone makes this an excellent piece to read aloud with students. This will also allow you to clarify some of the difficult vocabulary.	Have students *analyze* the ending of the story by creating an imaginary "timeline" of possible events that occurred as a result of Eckels's actions.	**Writing a Description:** Tell students that Bradbury is considered a master of descriptive language. Have them look closely at his description of the *Tyrannosaurus rex* on p. 71. What words bring the animal to life for the reader? Allow students time to write their own descriptions of a terrifying situation or creature, emulating Bradbury's style.

Vocabulary

aurora light; glow

correlate bring together; match

expendable replaceable; dispensable

mooring support; anchor

paradox contradiction; inconsistency

resilient flexible; springy

subliminal below conscious awareness

undulate rise and fall; ripple

Discussing the Short Story

1. What kind of hunting safaris does Time Safari, Inc. offer? (Recall) *The agency takes people into the past to hunt the animal of their choice.*

2. What precautions has Time Safari, Inc. taken to prevent changing the future? (Recall) *The travel agency has laid a path for the hunters to walk on and has marked for kill only those animals that are about to die anyway.*

3. Do you think Eckels's punishment for leaving the path was fair? (Analysis) *Some students will point out that Eckels was not aware of leaving the path, therefore, his punishment was too brutal. Others will argue that Eckels was warned repeatedly not to leave the path and ordered back to the Time Machine by both guides, therefore, he deserved his punishment.*

4. What do you think happened at the end of the story and why? (Analysis) *Most students will perceive that Travis killed Eckels because Eckels's actions significantly altered the future.*

Special Focus: The Chaos Theory

The idea that stepping on a butterfly can change the course of history is based on chaos theory. Developed by a meteorologist in 1960, chaos theory contends that complex and unpredictable results can occur from seemingly insignificant incidents. The most common example of this, known as the "Butterfly Effect," claims that the flapping of a butterfly's wings in Brazil can cause tiny atmospheric changes that can eventually cause a tornado in Texas. Use the following questions to discuss chaos theory.

- Some people argue that since the breeze created by a butterfly's wings is felt only 12–20 cm. away before it dissipates, the Butterfly Effect is not possible. What do you think?

- How might chaos theory explain ecological changes today, for example, the extinction of certain animals?

- If chaos theory holds true, what human activities might have "complex and unpredictable" results?

And They Lived Happily Ever After for a While

Poem

by John Ciardi, page 77

Summary

In a parody of a love poem, a couple living in a horribly polluted world declare their love for one another. They hold hands and await their deaths—which will come when their last oxygen tank runs out.

Reading Hint	Thinking Skill	Extension
Mention to students that both the title and the poem twist ordinarily pleasant words and images to give them negative meanings.	Ask students how far off they think Ciardi is in his description of the future.	**Revealing Names:** Have students make up place names to create different effects as Ciardi does in this poem. For example, what would they call a beach that is always overcrowded? A mountain with a high occurrence of avalanches? A river that floods every year? A school that wins (or loses) every sports event?

Discussing the Poem

1. What kind of world does the couple live in? (Recall) *They live in what seems to be a hopelessly polluted world.*

2. How long does the couple expect to live? (Recall) *They will live until their oxygen supply runs out.*

3. The poem is intended to be humorous but at the same time, Ciardi is sending a sad message. What is it? (Analysis) *Answers will vary. Ciardi's message might be that couples in love may not have the chance to spend a typical lifetime together if humans don't take better care of the earth.*

4. How does this vision of the future compare to the one in Rachel Carson's fable from *Silent Spring*? (Analysis) *Answers will vary. They are similar in that they both predict disaster, but some students may note that the tones and forms are very different.*

Literary Focus: Parody

Tell students that a *parody* is a humorous imitation of a particular style or work—usually one that is more serious. A parody is a form of satire, or humor intended to criticize. In this poem Ciardi parodies the style of love poetry. For example, Ciardi echoes Edgar Allan Poe's "Annabel Lee," which describes the love of a couple "in a kingdom by the sea." Here the couple falls in love "down by the Dirty River." Use the following to discuss parody.

- What is Ciardi criticizing in his poem?
- In what ways is Ciardi's poem similar to love poetry?
- How effective is his use of ugly images of nature? Point out specific examples.
- What famous painting is the accompanying image meant to parody?

What Happens When Humanity and Nature Collide?

Thinking Skill: ANALYZING

1. Using a chart such as the one below, analyze what happens in each of the following selections when humanity and nature collide. An example has been done for you.

Selection	Description of Collision and Result
A Fable for Tomorrow	man-made chemicals cause death of ecosystem
Battle for the Rain Forest	*the rain forest is destroyed and its inhabitants are displaced*
When Nature Comes Too Close	*people, pets, and the environment are threatened by an overabundance of wild animals*
All Revved Up About an Even Bigger Vehicle	*SUVs cause pollution, use a lot of gas, and are hazards to other drivers*
A Sound of Thunder	*the death of an insect changes the future*

2. In your opinion, what is the main point of "Battle for the Rain Forest"? **Analyzing** the needs and positions of native people, their governments, and foreign oil companies will help you decide. *Answers will vary. An analysis of needs might include some of the following. If native people have to give up their land, they should be compensated. The government's needs for the revenue from foreign oil companies overrides concern for the environment or indigenous people. The oil companies insist on being free from laws that hurt production. The foreign nations that buy the oil need it to maintain lifestyles. The essay shows that a simple society can be damaged by a distant nation. Although the author points out that native people can fight back, he predicts an ongoing confrontation as needs and values continue to clash.*

3. Discuss the debate topic: "American environmental and human-rights standards should apply to U.S. companies operating overseas." *Answers will vary. People working in third-world countries might accept American environmental and human-rights standards if they could keep their jobs. Yet some countries say that using American standards would make it impossible for them to compete in the marketplace. And U.S. companies often claim that operating in developing countries actually helps those countries. Environmentalists may say that the resulting environmental damage is serious, and holding companies to U.S. environmental standards must go hand-in-hand with human rights.*

4. The tone of a piece of writing is its mood or atmosphere. In "Wisdomkeepers" in cluster one, Oren Lyons conveys his philosophy in an angry tone. In one word each, how would you describe the tone of each selection in this cluster? *Answers will vary. Some suggestions follow: A Fable for Tomorrow—alarm, despair; All Revved Up About an Even Bigger Vehicle—humorous, annoyed; Battle for the Rain Forest—gloomy, angry; When Nature Comes Too Close—factual, powerless; A Sound of Thunder—frightened, worried; And They Lived Happily Ever After for a While—humorous, cynical.*

5. How does "A Sound of Thunder" illustrate chaos theory as it is described in the essay "Butterfly vs. Asteroid" on p. 9? *The essay includes a story about a butterfly in Brazil causing a tornado in Texas. According to chaos theory, sometimes "even very small actions can have very large consequences." In "The Sound of Thunder," stepping on a butterfly 60 million years in the past causes changes in the year 2055. The characters in the story discuss how a tiny change can produce major consequences.*

Writing Activity: Environmental Analysis

The handout on the next page provides a graphic organizer to help students with the writing activity. You may wish to use the Writing Activity Handout as an assessment. See also page 62 for a sample rubric to use with student essays and projects.

Writing Activity: Environmental Analysis

With **analysis** you break down a topic or subject into parts so that it is easier to understand. In an analysis essay, you put the parts back together to paint a picture of a topic or issue. Environmental issues can be complex. But if you identify from the selection and your own thinking reasons why the issue is important and possible solutions, you will begin to develop a clear picture of the issue you will write your analysis about.

Directions   Of the environmental issues explored in this cluster, choose the one that matters to you most. Then analyze why it is important and how it could be resolved, putting your thoughts into an analysis essay.

I. Review the selections and identify the issue you want to write about.

II. List at least three reasons why the issue is important.

A. _____

B. _____

C. _____

III. Write down at least three possible solutions to the problems the issue raises.

A. _____

B. _____

C. _____

IV. Now use the most significant reasons and solutions from the lists above in your analysis essay.

A Strong Analysis

- demonstrates careful examination of each part of the topic.
- supports each point with evidence.
- organizes information clearly.
- ends with a summary of the ideas presented.

Cluster Two Vocabulary Test

Vocabulary Words

Choose the meaning of the bold word in each passage.

1. Some evil spell had settled on the community: mysterious **maladies** swept the flocks of chickens . . . (*A Fable for Tomorrow, p. 48*)

   Ⓐ winds   Ⓑ spirits

   Ⓒ illnesses   Ⓓ powers

2. The few birds seen anywhere were **moribund**; they trembled violently and could not fly. (*A Fable for Tomorrow, p. 48*)

   Ⓐ dying   Ⓑ nervous

   Ⓒ depressed   Ⓓ tragic

3. And the Huaorani people—who are threatened with **eradication** of their culture for the sake of enough oil to meet U.S. energy needs for 10 days—have marched on Maxus Energy facilities. (*Battle for the Rain Forest, p. 52*)

   Ⓐ revolution   Ⓑ destruction

   Ⓒ rebirth   Ⓓ development

4. But oil companies have told the government they won't tolerate any laws that might **impede** production, and the government has not enforced them. (*Battle for the Rain Forest, p. 54*)

   Ⓐ block   Ⓑ encourage

   Ⓒ destroy   Ⓓ rush

5. This is America, darn it, and Chevrolet is not about to just sit by and watch Ford walk away with the **coveted** title of Least Sane Motor Vehicle. (*All Revved Up About an Even Bigger Vehicle, p. 58*)

   Ⓐ ridiculous   Ⓑ dreaded

   Ⓒ humorous   Ⓓ envied

6. Bear **proliferation**, meanwhile, has taken place all across the country. (*When Nature Comes Too Close, p. 61*)

   Ⓐ killing   Ⓑ relocation

   Ⓒ capture   Ⓓ population increase

7. [Coyotes are] also difficult to trap, and more so the older and **wilier** they become. (*When Nature Comes Too Close, p. 62*)

   Ⓐ grayer   Ⓑ weaker

   Ⓒ trickier   Ⓓ angrier

8. "That'd be a **paradox**," said the latter. "Time doesn't permit that sort of mess—a man meeting himself." (*A Sound of Thunder, p. 70*)

   Ⓐ mistake   Ⓑ joke

   Ⓒ tragedy   Ⓓ contradiction

9. It came on great oiled, **resilient**, striding legs. (*A Sound of Thunder, p. 71*)

   Ⓐ flexible   Ⓑ powerful

   Ⓒ long   Ⓓ muscular

10. In the slime, tiny insects wriggled, so that the entire body seemed to twitch and **undulate**, even while the monster itself did not move. (*A Sound of Thunder, p. 72*)

    Ⓐ jerk   Ⓑ ripple

    Ⓒ bend   Ⓓ swerve

CLUSTER THREE

Problem Solving

I. Present this definition to students.

For **problem solving** you use a series of thinking skills.

- Define the problem.
- Gather information about the problem.
- Brainstorm possible solutions, then evaluate each possibility.
- Select a course of action based on your information and evaluations.
- Check to see how well the course of action is working.
- Redefine the problem or identify additional problems, and start the process over.

II. Discuss with students how they already use problem solving by sharing the situations below.

You use problem solving when

- you get people with differing opinions to cooperate on a school project.
- you decide whether to use your hard-earned money for a computer, a used car, or a college savings account.
- you work out a schedule so that you can get your work done and still have time for recreation.
- you work out the quickest way to get from one place to another.

Ask students to suggest other situations where problem solving would be used.

III. Explain to students that they will be given a description of a problem that they will read about in more depth in a selection in Cluster Three, "David Meets Goliath at City Hall."

A. Use the reproducible "Solving a Problem" on page 35 as an overhead transparency or blackline master.

B. Go over the series of thinking skills used to solve a problem.

C. Either place students in small groups or have them work independently.

D. Instruct students to refer to the thinking skills to develop a list of steps they would take to solve the problem outlined. Tell them to list the steps in the space labelled "My Plan."

E. Go over each plan. Ask the class to decide which steps they think would work best. Merge these steps into a final plan.

F. Suggest that after students read the selection, "David Meets Goliath at City Hall," they come back to this activity and compare their solutions to the one that was actually used in the selection.

Solving a Problem

Cluster Question: How Can We Live in Harmony with Nature?

Definition: In problem solving you use a series of thinking skills.

- Define the problem
- Gather information about the problem.
- Brainstorm possible solutions, then evaluate each possibility.
- Select a course of action based on your information and evaluations.
- Check to see how well the course of action is working.
- Redefine the problem or identify additional problems, and start the process over.

Directions: Below is a description of a problem faced by 12-year-old Andrew Holleman in "David Meets Goliath at City Hall," a selection in this cluster. Referring to the series of thinking skills above, list the steps you might take to solve this problem. Then, as a class, go over each plan. Decide which steps would work best. Only six steps are listed below; add more as necessary.

> **Problem:** Twelve-year-old Andrew Holleman's parents receive a notice stating that a real estate developer plans to turn the local woods near their town into a condominium complex. The notice states that a public meeting to discuss the developer's plan will be held at the town hall. Andrew sees the situation as problematic because it will destroy the habitat of the animals that live in the woods and it will deprive naturalists of a place to go to study a nature habitat.

My plan:

Step 1: _____

_____

Step 2: _____

_____

Step 3: _____

_____

Step 4: _____

_____

Step 5: _____

_____

Step 6: _____

_____

Cluster Three Vocabulary

Watch for the following words as you read the selections in Cluster Three. Record your own vocabulary words and definitions on the blank lines.

Heroes for the Planet: Then and Now
pages 80–83

denuded made bare; exposed

_____

_____

The Sun pages 84–85

billowing surging; swelling
imperial majestic; royal
rumpled wrinkled; disordered

_____

_____

A Palace of Bird Beaks pages 86–89

_____

_____

The Face of a Spider pages 90–95

adroitly skillfully; cleverly
aesthetic pleasing to the senses
countenance face; appearance
gossamer delicate; sheer
rancor ill will; malice
sanctioned allowed; authorized
squandered wasted; neglected to use
vigilantly watchfully; attentively

_____

_____

David Meets Goliath At City Hall
pages 96–100

abutted bordered; connected to
declining disappearing; vanishing
magnitude size; immensity
petition appeal; request
sited located; positioned
sound firm; durable
withstand survive; endure

_____

_____

Animals, Vegetables and Minerals
pages 101–104

complement add to; complete
dispel get rid of
fluke accident; chance occurrence
grossly outrageously; totally
priorities preferences; ranking of ideas

_____

_____

Working against Time page 105

aslant sideways
splayed spread outward

_____

_____

The King of the Beasts pages 106–107

radiate glow; beam
wantonly carelessly; recklessly

_____

_____

Heroes for the Planet: Then and Now

Photo Essay

by Time Magazine, pages 80–83

Summary

Using photographs and brief descriptions, this essay contrasts environmentally harmful industrial practices with improved methods that help protect the environment or reclaim damaged areas. In each case, a caveat, or warning, indicates limitations of the effectiveness of the improved methods.

Reading Hint	Thinking Skill	Extension
Inform students that "caveat" is from a Latin word meaning "let him beware." A caveat is a word of caution that further explains a statement or situation.	Ask students what other environmental problems not addressed in the photo essay have already been improved or could still be improved.	**Redefining Problems:** Each caveat indicates a new problem to be solved. Use the caveats to discuss this part of the problem-solving process with students. How would students define the problem indicated by each caveat? How would they begin gathering the necessary information to work out a solution to that problem?

Vocabulary

denuded made bare; exposed

Discussing the Photo Essay

1. What initially caused the problems covered by the "then" parts of the photo essay? (Recall) *The problems described were caused by industrial practices that were harmful to the environment.*

2. Why do you think the improved environmental practices featured in this photo essay are said to be the work of heroes? (Analysis) *Answers will vary. Some students may feel that it is admirable for an industry to become a leader in developing more environmentally friendly methods. Others may offer that those same industries caused the problems and are only doing what they should to correct matters.*

3. Why do you think the improved methods are not immediately adopted by every industry that could use them? (Analysis) *Answers will vary. Students may point out that changing industrial methods can be very expensive and that a company may become non-competitive if it is the only one making changes.*

Special Focus: Photojournalism

During the American Civil War, photographers began to record battlefield scenes. Soon after, early photojournalists photographed the effects of natural disasters such as tornadoes and floods. Since then, photojournalists have revealed the living conditions of the poor and the plight of immigrants. They have documented factories' terrible labor conditions, World War I battlefield scenes, and the struggles of families during the Great Depression.

Discuss photojournalism with your students, using the following questions.

- Why are pictures sometimes more powerful than words?
- How can photographs be used to affect public opinion?
- Which photograph in this essay do you find most effective? Why?

The Sun by Mary Oliver, pages 84–85

Poem

Summary

The poem describes the sun as gentle, noble, helpful, and beautiful. The speaker asks if it's possible to adequately express the pleasure the sun brings us. Or, the speaker asks, has the reader turned away from nature and gone mad over power and things?

Reading Hint	Thinking Skill	Extension
Point out that this poem is written as one long question addressed to the reader.	Ask students to identify the *problem* implied by the last six lines of the poem.	**Appreciating Nature:** "The Sun" implies that people who have "turned from this world" are missing a lot. Ask students how they feel about this message. Are people who are sensitive to nature's beauties happier or better off? If turning away from nature is a problem, what are some possible solutions?

Vocabulary

billowing surging; swelling

imperial majestic; royal

rumpled wrinkled; disordered

Discussing the Poem

1. How is the sun characterized in the poem? (Analysis) *Answers will vary. The sun is characterized as beautiful, warming, majestic, and helpful.*

2. In what way does the speaker question the limitations of the English language? (Recall) *She wonders if the English language can adequately express all the virtues of the sun.*

3. In what way does the speaker challenge readers? (Analysis) *The speaker asks whether readers appreciate the sun, or whether they have, instead, turned away from the natural world and gone mad for power and for things.*

Special Focus: Images of a Powerful Sun

Tell students that the sun plays an important role in the traditions of virtually every culture. In the Japanese Shinto tradition, the sun is the most beautiful of the deities—the goddess Amaterasu. In Greek mythology, the sun god Helios drives his chariot across the heavens each day, causing the sunrise. In Native American Hopi stories, the sun god Tawa co-creates the world with the earth goddess Spider Woman.

Science fiction writers sometimes envision a world without the sun's warmth. Even today psychologists use powerful lamps to combat seasonal affective disorder, a condition that results from too little sunlight. Discuss with your students the idea of the sun as a psychological force by using the following questions.

- Do you feel noticeably different on cloudy days than on sunny days?

- In what situations might the power of the sun be less welcome than it is described to be in the poem?

- List some adjectives, verbs, and figures of speech that would express the sun as being uncomfortable, dangerous, or destructive. Compare and contrast your descriptive words with those used in the poem.

- If you were to depict or describe the sun in a poem or painting of your own, would it be like or unlike the sun described in the poem? Explain your answer.

A Palace of Bird Beaks   by Howard Schwartz and Barbara Rush, pages 86–89   Folk Tale

Summary

When King Solomon's wife requests a palace built of bird beaks for her birthday, the king summons all the birds to contribute. The little hoopoe bird pleads for the king to answer three riddles before debeaking the birds. The riddles lead the king to greater insight into the consequences of his proposed action—and to a change of mind.

Reading Hint	Thinking Skill	Extension
Inform students that the historical King Solomon was the king of Israel from about 972–922 BC. Tales of Solomon's wisdom appear in the Bible as well as in the folklore of other cultures.	Ask your students to describe and discuss the *problem-solving* technique that the hoopoe bird uses in this story.	**Using Subtlety:** Point out to students that the king now faces a new problem: he must tell the queen that her wish will not be granted. Have them create a dialogue in which the king uses the same subtle approach with the queen that the hoopoe bird used with him.

Discussing the Folk Tale

1. Why does King Solomon's wife ask for a palace made out of bird beaks? (Recall) *For her birthday, she wants "something that no other queen on earth has ever had."*

2. Why does the hoopoe bird present Solomon with three riddles? (Analysis) *Answers will vary. The hoopoe wants to cause Solomon to think more clearly about the issue and, therefore, to reach a more desirable conclusion for the birds.*

3. According to this story, how did hoopoe birds get their distinctive head feathers? (Recall) *Solomon rewards the hoopoe with a small crown much like the one that the king himself wears. The implication is that all hoopoes since that time have worn a crest of feathers.*

4. How does the hoopoe get Solomon to change his mind about making a palace of bird beaks? (Analysis) *Instead of begging or demanding, he subtly allows Solomon to see the injustice of what he is seeking. He asks questions to make his point.*

Special Focus: A Modern-Day Moral

Tell students that situations are created in folk tales to teach a moral. In this story, many birds are about to lose their beaks to satisfy the whims of a selfish queen. Use the following question to prompt discussion.

- What are three possible morals of this story? *Answers will vary. Possible morals include:*
  - *A king should never be too proud to admit he has made a mistake.*
  - *It is sometimes necessary to speak up, even to a person in authority.*
  - *People should not request gifts that could hurt others.*
- What other stories have you read in this book so far that would lend themselves well to a folk tale treatment?
- What might the morals of these stories be?

The Face of a Spider by David Quammen, pages 90–95   Essay

Summary

David Quammen discovers about 100 baby black widow spiders running around on his desk. His reflections on possible solutions to the problem lead him into the larger question, "How should a human behave toward the members of other species?" His suggestion: make eye contact with the creature before deciding what to do.

Reading Hint	Thinking Skill	Extension
Point out to students that Quammen is focusing on a small incident in order to consider a larger philosophical problem.	Ask students to *define the problems*—the first problem and the underlying major problem—raised by the essay. Would they have considered these issues in the same situation?	**Considering the Alternatives:** Ask students to consider several possible solutions to Quammen's spider problem. Which one would they have chosen?

Vocabulary

adroitly skillfully; cleverly

aesthetic pleasing to the senses

countenance face; appearance

gossamer delicate; sheer

rancor ill will; malice

sanctioned allowed; authorized

squandered wasted; neglected to use

vigilantly watchfully; attentively

Discussing the Essay

1. What immediate problem faces the author when he returns to his office? (Recall) *About 100 baby black widow spiders are running around on his desk.*

2. Why does the situation lead Quammen to think beyond his immediate problem to the question of how we should treat other species? (Analysis) *Answers will vary. Students may say that Quammen is already interested in such issues. Others may say that any troubling ethical situation leads one to philosophize.*

3. What does the author suggest people do before deciding how to treat another species? (Recalls) *He suggests that people make eye contact with the other creature first.*

4. How does Quammen feel about his solution to the spider problem? (Recall) *Quammen says that he has a lingering suspicion that he may have wasted an opportunity for moral growth.*

Special Focus: The Jain Religion

Tell students that people of the Jain religion of India believe it is wrong to harm any living creature. A true Jain does not burn a candle if there is a danger that a moth or other insect might fly into the flame. A Jain does not light a fire for heating or cooking for the same reason. A Jain would not cut his or her hair because the scissors might injure any lice hiding in the hair. A Jain would not plow a field for fear of hurting worms. Jains might even wear a cloth mask to avoid inhaling gnats. Discuss the Jainism perspective with students using the following questions.

- Is the principle of the Jain religion practical? Why or why not?
- How would your lives change if you became Jains?
- What might be a compromise between Jainism and your beliefs?

David Meets Goliath at City Hall by Andrew Holleman, pages 96–100   Article

Summary

When he read that the local woods were going to be turned into a condominium complex, 12-year-old Andrew Holleman went into action. He gathered information, wrote a petition, and aroused community interest in the problem. The building project was canceled, proving that sometimes you *can* fight city hall—even at the age of 12.

Reading Hint	Thinking Skill	Extension
Be sure students are familiar with the biblical story in which the young David, armed only with a sling, defeats the giant Goliath.	Ask students to identify the parts of the article in which the author *defines the problem* and *gathers information.*	**David vs. Goliath Stories:** Have students go back through the clusters they've read so far. How many selections could be defined as "David vs. Goliath" stories? Why is such a stand-off particularly common when dealing with ecological issues?

Vocabulary

abutted bordered; connected to

declining disappearing; vanishing

magnitude size; immensity

petition appeal; request

sited located; positioned

sound firm; durable

withstand survive; endure

Discussing the Article

1. What steps did Holleman take to solve his problem? (Recall) *He gathered information on the situation, circulated a petition that caught the interest of many people, and made a speech at a meeting on the topic. He wrote letters to politicians and news people and got the advice of a biologist from the Audubon Society. He and others formed a neighborhood association to keep people informed.*

2. Why do you think there was so much community interest in the situation? (Analysis) *Answers will vary. Like Andrew, many members of the community must have cared about what happened to the natural area that was about to be developed. Others may have been motivated by more general environmental concerns or may have been caught up in the enthusiasm and "joined the bandwagon."*

3. Was the appeal Andrew made logical or emotional, or both? Give examples for your answer. (Analysis) *Answers will vary. Andrew made both kinds of appeals. He gathered data for logical arguments. He also used the shell of a wood turtle and his personal testimony in an emotional appeal.*

Special Focus: You Can't Fight City Hall

Tell students that a *cliché* is an overused expression. "You can't fight city hall" is a cliché that has been popular in this country for generations. The phrase means that the government is indifferent to the concerns of its citizens, and so the common person—especially a lone individual—has little chance of bringing about change. Use questions such as the following to discuss the idea of "fighting city hall."

- Holleman was told that "the developer was a 'townie' who always got his way." What kind of difficulty does this imply for Holleman's efforts?
- What was Holleman's response to the advice that he couldn't fight city hall?
- Identify a problem in your community. How difficult do you think it would be to solve?

Animals, Vegetables and Minerals
by Jessica Szymczyk, pages 101–104

Personal Opinion

Summary
Jessica Szymczyk, a long-time animal lover, claims that most people have misconceptions about the use of animals in research. Animals used in testing do not have to suffer, she says, and the research is necessary in that it improves life for humans and animals alike.

Reading Hint	Thinking Skill	Extension
Before they read this selection, have students jot down their impressions of an animal research lab.	What *problems* might public attitude cause for animal research labs? How might these labs change public attitude?	**Both Sides:** Ask one group to brainstorm a list of the beliefs and arguments of those in favor of animal research; the other group to brainstorm a list for those opposed. Reunite the students and compare lists.

Vocabulary

complement add to; complete

dispel get rid of

fluke accident; chance occurrence

grossly outrageously; totally

priorities preferences; ranking of ideas

Discussing the Personal Opinion

1. How does the author's description of the lab she works in differ from the impressions you noted before reading the selection? (Analysis) *Answers will vary.*

2. As an animal lover, how does the author justify working at such a lab? (Recall) *Szymczyk says that the animals are well-treated and that the work is very important to society.*

3. Do you detect any contradictions between Jessica's love of animals and her job? (Analysis) *Answers will vary. Some students may note that the animals are not volunteers, that at least some of the tests have to produce painful results, and that some animals are killed after an experiment.*

4. Has this selection changed your attitude toward research that uses animals? Explain. (Analysis) *Answers will vary.*

Special Focus: The Animal Testing Debate

Animals are used in laboratory experiments for many purposes. Health-care products must be tested to meet the safety requirements of the U.S. Food and Drug Administration. Drugs, cosmetics, and medical devices are tested on animals, as well as the effects of tobacco smoke.

Researchers are seeking alternative methods, including cell and tissue culture and computer modeling. Meanwhile, strict guidelines are imposed on government-funded research projects. Use the following questions to discuss the problems of animal research.

- Do animals have rights? If so, define them. If not, why not?
- Should limits be set on the types of experiments permitted on animals? If so, where would you draw the line? For example, is the use of animals to test cosmetics as valid as testing drugs that might save human lives?
- If animals do have rights, does that bring up other issues such as whether they should be kept in zoos or used for food, work, or recreation?

Working against Time   by David Wagoner, page 105   Poem

Summary
The speaker discovers that young hemlock trees have been uprooted by bulldozers to make a logging road. Hurriedly, he digs some up, stuffs them in his car, takes them home, and plants them. Two survive.

Reading Hint	Thinking Skill	Extension
Draw students' attention to footnotes explaining words that may be unfamiliar.	When the speaker discovers what's happened, it is almost too late to save the trees. How could the problems in the poem have been prevented?	**Other Points of View:** The speaker in the poem is an environmentalist. How would the developer of the land or the operator of the bulldozer view the situation? Have students write a poem about the incident from one of these points of view.

Vocabulary
aslant sideways

splayed spread outward

Discussing the Poem

1. What has happened to the young trees that the speaker finds? (Recall) *They have been uprooted by a bulldozer making a logging road.*

2. Why does the speaker take some of the trees home? (Recall) *He wants to replant them so they might live.*

3. What do you think the speaker's attitude is toward the loggers who bulldozed the road? (Analysis) *Answers may vary. Although the poem contains no judgmental statements, it's obvious from the poet's actions that he doesn't think trees should be carelessly killed. He says that he was the only one "singing in the woods," which may be intended as a comment on the scene. He also notes, perhaps with a bit of irony, that "It's against the law to dig up trees."*

4. Do you think the speaker feels afterwards that his effort was worthwhile? (Analysis) *Answers may vary. As he starts home with the trees, he's singing. Many students may feel that the last lines indicate a feeling of satisfaction.*

Literary Focus: Poetry and Prose
Poetry can usually be told from prose simply by the way it looks. When writing poetry, an author emphasizes the composition of the line, rather than the sentence.

"Working against Time" is divided into four stanzas of six lines each, rather than into paragraphs. But it has no rhyme, and its meter is irregular. Suggest that students read the poem aloud to understand how this loose poetic form follows the rhythm of speech. Or, you might read it aloud to them.

Point out that some lines have no pause at the end. For example, "their branches crammed / Into each other's light." Ask students to find other run-on lines and read them aloud.

Ask students to rewrite some or all of this piece in prose sentences and paragraphs. They might change some words and phrases to make the prose clearer. Use the following questions to prompt discussion.
- Does the form make a difference in the telling of this story? How
- Why do you think the author chose to use a poetic form rather than prose?
- Which form would you use for this kind of story? Why?

The King of the Beasts by Philip José Farmer, pages 106–107   Short Story

Summary

A biologist shows a distinguished visitor around a zoo and a scientific laboratory. In the lab, extinct species such as giraffes, gorillas, and sea otters are being re-created for display in the zoo. But the biologist's prize specimen—the most dangerous species of all—is a man.

Reading Hint	Thinking Skill	Extension
This would be an excellent selection to read aloud. As you do so, instruct students to note when and how their perceptions of what is taking place in the story change.	Have students *analyze* why Farmer chose to delay revealing key elements of the story until the very end.	**Do We Have a Future?** This story implies that humans will someday be extinct. Ask your students to discuss ways humans might bring about their own extinction. What other things could cause the extinction of humans? Are any of them avoidable?

Vocabulary

radiate glow; beam

wantonly carelessly; recklessly

Discussing the Short Story

1. Where and when do you think the story is taking place? (Recall) *Students are likely to offer that the setting is in the distant future in a scientific laboratory either on the earth or on another planet.*

2. Why do you think the biologist is bringing back only one human being? (Analysis) *Answers will vary. By bringing back a single individual, the biologist avoids the possibility of them reproducing. Since humans were so destructive, it may be feared that they would be so again if the race were allowed to thrive.*

3. What connection can you make between this story and other selections in the anthology? (Analysis) *Answers will vary. Some students may feel that this story shows the long-term results of conditions suggested in "A Fable for Tomorrow," "When Nature Comes Too Close," and "They Lived Happily Ever After for a While."*

Special Focus: Re-Creating a Species

Long a popular idea in science fiction stories, the recreation of extinct creatures may actually be possible. For example, cloning has been used to reproduce some of today's plants and animals. For cloning, biologists use cells from an animal such as a sheep to "grow" one or more copies of that animal. The "clones" have exactly the same characteristics as the source of the genetic material. Genetic material from extinct species, if accessible, could presumably be used to bring these species back to life. Use questions such as the following to discuss artificial re-creation of species.

- Do you think that a species should be re-created once it becomes extinct? Why or why not?
- How should biologists decide what species to bring back?
- What might happen if we released long extinct species into the environment?
- How might humanity benefit from bringing back extinct species?

How Can We Live in Harmony with Nature?

Thinking Skill: PROBLEM SOLVING

1. "A picture is worth a thousand words," according to one old saying. Imagine that you are the editor of an ecology magazine who is developing an issue focused on any of the ecological problems described so far in this book. Describe the photograph you would put on the cover to draw readers' attention to the problem. *Answers will vary. Students might bring in examples from magazines or newspapers of images they would like to use.*

2. In "Animals, Vegetables and Minerals," Jessica Szymczyk tells readers that although animals should be treated with kindness and respect, in matters such as medical research there is no question that humans come first. Explain why you agree or disagree. *Answers will vary. According to Oren Lyons, all life is equal. In "The Face of a Spider," David Quammen discusses the Jain religion's view of equality between species. Students might want to discuss why we especially value human lives.*

3. **Arachnophobia** means "fear of spiders." Why do you think some people are afraid of creatures such as spiders, bats, and snakes? *Answers will vary. Such reactions might be based on stories we have heard or the ways we have seen other people react. We also might fear creatures that are very different from human beings or that seem especially "creepy."*

4. The title of "David Meets Goliath at City Hall" obviously refers to the biblical story of David and Goliath. In what ways is author Andrew Holleman like David and the land developers like Goliath? *Like David, Andrew Holleman is young, relatively small, and an underdog, but he is surprisingly good with the "weapons" he brings into play. Like Goliath, City Hall represents those who are older, accustomed to being in charge, and more experienced in battle.*

Writing Activity: Future World Scenario

The handout on page 46 provides a graphic organizer to help students with the writing activity. You may wish to use the Writing Activity Handout as an assessment. See also page 62 for a sample rubric to use with student essays and projects.

Writing Activity: Future World Scenario

Science fiction writers often create future societies based on one or two simple premises or "what if?" questions. For example, a writer might ask the question, "What would happen if people lost contact with nature because they never went outside?" Or "What would happen if pollution dramatically changed the world's climate?" The writer then uses that premise as the basis of a story.

   With a partner, come up with a premise based on one or more environmental issue(s). Then use that premise to create a scenario or plot outline for a short story.

Premise or **"What if?"** _____

_____

Scene or **setting** _____

_____

_____

Plot (What happens first? What follows?) _____

1. _____

_____

2. _____

_____

3. _____

_____

4. _____

_____

5. _____

_____

Conclusion (How does the story end?) _____

_____

_____

A future world scenario
- presents the premise or "what if?" question.
- shows the impact the problem is having on the world or society.
- outlines a series of events (plot).
- bring matters to a crisis and conclusion.
- often goes on to serve as the basis of a more complete piece of writing, such as a short story or script.

Cluster Three Vocabulary Test

Vocabulary Words

Choose the meaning of the bold word in each passage.

1. Clear-cutting and hauling left hills **denuded** and scarred by logging roads. (*Heroes for the Planet Then and Now, p. 82*)

   Ⓐ closed   Ⓑ rough
   Ⓒ made bare   Ⓓ rocky

2. . . . say, on a morning in early summer, at its perfect **imperial** distance— (*The Sun, p. 84*)

   Ⓐ typical   Ⓑ viewing
   Ⓒ required   Ⓓ majestic

3. I knew she would have to be either murdered or else captured **adroitly**. . . (*The Face of a Spider, p. 92*)

   Ⓐ cruelly   Ⓑ skillfully
   Ⓒ in isolation   Ⓓ permanently

4. She had laid her eggs into a silken egg sac the size of a Milk Dud and then protected that sac **vigilantly**. . . (*The Face of a Spider, p. 92*)

   Ⓐ enthusiastically   Ⓑ murderously
   Ⓒ watchfully   Ⓓ lazily

5. . . . [T]he developer had sent his original notification to the 50 families whose homes **abutted** the property. (*David Meets Goliath at City Hall, p. 98*)

   Ⓐ divided   Ⓑ overlapped
   Ⓒ covered   Ⓓ bordered

6. Don't ever give up the fight against a poorly **sited** development, pollution, or anything environmentally dangerous. (*David Meets Goliath at City Hall, p. 99*)

   Ⓐ elevated   Ⓑ designed
   Ⓒ built   Ⓓ located

7. . . . [T]hey are also **grossly** mistaken about my colleagues, our work and the conditions under which we keep our animals. (*Animals, Vegetables and Minerals, p. 101*)

   Ⓐ totally   Ⓑ sadly
   Ⓒ slightly   Ⓓ heavily

8. I want to **dispel** any idea that I do what I do for the money. (*Animals, Vegetables and Minerals, p. 102*)

   Ⓐ get rid of   Ⓑ expose
   Ⓒ consider   Ⓓ support

9. Test duplications are sometimes needed to show that the results of the first study aren't a **fluke**. (*Animals, Vegetables and Minerals, p. 103*)

   Ⓐ accident   Ⓑ joke
   Ⓒ exaggeration   Ⓓ lie

10. "So we bring to life only the higher animals, the beautiful ones that were **wantonly** exterminated." (*The King of the Beasts, p. 106*)

    Ⓐ rapidly   Ⓑ recklessly
    Ⓒ gradually   Ⓓ accidentally

Teaching Cluster Four

The final cluster in *What on Earth?* can be presented using one or more of the following methods.

- presented by the teacher
- used for independent student learning
- used for a final assessment

Use the chart below to plan.

Teacher Presentation	Independent Learning/Assessment
For teacher-directed study you can • pass out cluster vocabulary sheet. • set schedule for reading selections. • use appropriate discussion questions and extension activities for each selection. • administer vocabulary test. • assign research projects. • administer final essay test.	**Students can** • plan and present a lesson over one or more of the selections in the last cluster. • prepare a vocabulary study sheet and create and administer a vocabulary test. • conduct additional research on a related topic. • respond to one or more of the questions or activities on the Responding to Cluster Four page.

Teacher Notes

CLUSTER FOUR

Synthesizing

I. Present this definition to students.

Synthesizing means combining parts into a new whole.

II. Discuss with students how they already use synthesis by sharing the situations below.

You use synthesis when you
- use what you already know to figure out the meaning of a new word.
- combine several brainstorming suggestions to develop a solution to a problem.
- develop a consensus of opinion based on everyone's ideas.
- use information from several different sources in a project.
- adapt an idea from one form to another (for example, you create a play based on a novel or a dance based on a poem).

Ask students to suggest other situations where synthesis would be used.

III. Explain to students that they will use synthesis to create a wise saying, or *maxim*, based on one of the selections they have already read. Use the following steps to show how to synthesize.

A. Use the reproducible "Ecology Maxims" on page 50 as an overhead transparency or black-line master.

B. Show how one reader created a maxim based on the quotation in the selection "A Fable for Tomorrow." Point out that synthesizing is a higher-order thinking skill that often requires other thinking skills such as analysis (to find a quotation that reflects one or more of the ideas in a piece) and summarizing (to rephrase the main idea).

C. Have students review the selections they have already read—perhaps by looking over the table of contents on pages 6–8 of the book. Then have them select a piece with which they want to work. Using **Organizer A** as a model, have them complete **Organizer B**. If necessary, prompt students with one or more of the following questions.
- What is the main idea of the piece you have selected?
- What was the ecological situation in the selection?
- Do you remember a key phrase or event from the piece? Students may need to skim their selections to find a meaningful quotation or to refresh their memories about the event.

Finally, give students time to write their maxims.

D. When your students have completed the activity, they have begun to synthesize an answer to the essential question "How Do We Protect Our Planet?"

Ecology Maxims

Essential Question: How Do We Protect Our Planet?

Definition: Synthesizing means combining parts into a new whole.

A *maxim* is a wise saying or short statement about a topic. You may be familiar with Benjamin Franklin's rhyming maxim "An apple a day keeps the doctor away." Not all maxims rhyme, however. The following example, particularly appropriate for this book, was written by Henry David Thoreau: "In wildness is the preservation of the world." Another maxim on ecology is by Al Bernstein: "We treat this world of ours as if we had a spare in the trunk."

In a sense, a maxim is a type of synthesis or summary statement on a topic. A maxim condenses a complex situation into a short statement full of wisdom and experience. What maxims can you develop about ecology and the environment now that you have read several clusters of stories and articles?

Directions: Organizer A shows an example of a maxim based on "A Fable for Tomorrow" from the second cluster. Notice how the author of the maxim first located an interesting quotation from the selection and then summarized the quotation to create the saying. Other maxims could be created from the same quotation. Now review the selections you have read so far in this book. Select one that you think would yield a wise saying.

Use **Organizer B** to record a situation or quotation from your selection and your ecology maxim.

Organizer A   Selection: A Fable for Tomorrow from *Silent Spring*

Quotation/Situation	Ecology Maxim
No witchcraft, no enemy action had silenced the rebirth of new life in this stricken world. The people had done it themselves.	We cannot blame ecological problems on others—we are own worst enemies.

Organizer B   Selection: _____

Quotation/Situation	Ecology Maxim

Cluster Four Vocabulary

Watch for the following words as you read the selections in Cluster Four. Record your own vocabulary words and definitions in the blank lines.

A Young Environmentalist Speaks Out
pages 110–112

agenda plan; program
delegates representatives; members

_____

_____

_____

The Mushroom pages 113–117

consecrated declared sacred; blessed
fruiting reproducing; multiplying
memoirs personal history; personal memories
indifferent unconcerned; unfeeling
inexorably inescapably; unavoidably
infidels disbelievers; doubters
infinite endless; eternal
secreted discharged; emitted
sheath outer layer; case
successor replacement; follower

_____

_____

_____

Duck Hunting pages 118–123

_____

_____

_____

The Last Dog pages 124–137

copious plentiful; abundant
cull gather; pick out
evasive vague; unspecific
forays invasions; raids
interfacing interacting; connecting
languishing drooping; fading
objectivity fairness; neutrality
provocation prompting; motive
reproof scolding; disapproval
tentatively uncertainly; hesitantly

_____

_____

_____

Is the Weather Getting Worse?
pages 138–141

albeit although; even if
benign kind; mild
expositions explanations; speeches
induced caused; created
inundated flooded; overwhelmed
ominous threatening; forbidding
uninhibited unstopped; unchecked
versatile clever; able to do many things
vicariously through another; indirectly

_____

_____

_____

The Last Street page 142

_____

_____

_____

A Young Environmentalist Speaks Out

Speech

by Severn Cullis-Suzuki, pages 110–112

Summary

Twelve-year-old Severn Cullis-Suzuki presented this speech to environmental experts and delegates from countries around the world. In it, she expresses her fears about the future of the earth's resources and creatures, including human beings.

Reading Hint	Thinking Skill	Extension
Let students know that the author was 12 years old when she delivered this speech at a session of Earth Summit in Rio de Janeiro in June of 1992.	With students, *analyze* Severn's speech for effectiveness. How does she appeal to her audience's emotions? to their sense of logic? of decency? What emotion do students think Severn aroused most in her audience?	**Applying a Wise Saying:** Ralph Waldo Emerson once said, "What you do speaks so loud that I cannot hear what you say." Find some examples of actions that speak louder than words in Severn's speech.

Vocabulary

agenda plan; program

delegates representatives; members

Discussing the Speech

1. What does the speaker mean when she says she is fighting for her future? (Recall) *She is afraid to go out into the sun because of the holes in the ozone and is afraid to breathe the air because of the chemicals that pollute it.*

2. Why does Severn think that being able to comfort children with phrases like "Everything's going to be all right" and "It's not the end of the world" is so important? (Analysis) *Answers will vary. Being able to use such phrases honestly indicates that there is a future.*

3. What effect do you think the phrase, "each of you is somebody's child" has on the audience? (Analysis) *Answers will vary. The use of such wording brings the issue down to a personal level, allowing Severn's listeners to better relate to what she is saying.*

4. Where does Severn suggest we find the money to solve environmental problems? (Recall) *Severn proposes that the money spent on war be used to solve environmental problems.*

Special Focus: Extinction

In this selection, the 12-year-old speaker expresses concern that animals alive now will be extinct by the time she has children. Yet preventing extinction can be a tricky business, as evidenced by the controversy over the Northern Spotted Owl in the 1980s. Environmental activists claimed that logging in Oregon was destroying the owl's habitat, leading to its extinction. Some "ecoterrorists" went to extremes, destroying logging company equipment and U.S. Forest Service property, inserting spikes into trees to shatter saw blades—blinding and injuring mill workers in the process—and chaining themselves to trees. The federal government began to restrict logging in the area, causing the closing of numerous mills. Use the following questions to prompt discussion.

- In your opinion, is the saving of a species from extinction justified if it puts people out of work or causes an industry to lose money?
- What do you think happens to an ecosystem when a species becomes extinct?
- Do you think the earth is resilient enough to withstand extinctions caused by humans?

The Mushroom by H. M. Hoover, pages 113–117 Essay

Summary

This essay describes the growth of a mushroom in North America from 450 A.D. to the present. Each stage is related to events in history, the most recent of which is the opening of a shopping mall built on land where many mushrooms were growing—with dire consequences for the shopping mall.

Reading Hint	Thinking Skill	Extension
Point out how the author threads actual historical personalities and events through the story of the mushroom's life.	Have students decide which scenarios in the essay are fact and which are fiction. Ask them to *analyze* why the author includes the fictional material?	**Writing Science Fiction:** Most readers will find the information about the mushroom mind-boggling. Ask students how this information might be used as a basis for a science fiction story.

Vocabulary

consecrated declared sacred; blessed

fruiting reproducing; multiplying

memoirs personal history; personal memories

indifferent unconcerned; unfeeling

inexorably inescapably; unavoidably

infidels disbelievers; doubters

infinite endless; eternal

secreted discharged; emitted

sheath outer layer; case

successor replacement; follower

Discussing the Essay

1. When the Europeans landed in America, how long had America's forests been evolving into perfect ecosystems, and how long did it take settlers to destroy much of the forest? (Recall) *America's forests had been evolving for 10,000 years, and it took only 200 years for America's settlers to destroy most of them.*

2. What is the author implying when she says that in earlier times humans walked over the mushroom in their moccasins but "left no footprints." (Analysis) *Answers will vary. She may be pointing out that American Indians trod lightly and respectfully on the earth, leaving it basically unchanged.*

3. Why do you think the author repeats the line, "A sheath of a thousand hyphae is no thicker than a human hair"? (Analysis) *Answers will vary. Some students may say she is pointing out that even the tiniest organisms become powerful when they multiply.*

Special Focus: People vs. Nature—Who Will Win?

Share these mind-boggling facts about nature with students before discussing the questions that follow.

- In 1980, the blast of ash, rock, and gasses caused by the eruption of Mount St. Helens traveled at speeds up to 675 mph and stripped trees from hillsides as far away as six miles.
- In 1992, Hurricane Andrew resulted in $25 billion in damage.
- In the 14th century, the bubonic plague killed nearly three quarters of the population in Europe and Asia.

Discuss the following with students.

- In what ways do humans attempt to keep nature under control?
- How do efforts to control nature sometimes backfire and threaten human existence?
- Do you think there will ever come a time when humans will completely control nature? If so, what will lead to that ability? If not, why not?

Duck Hunting by Gary Paulsen, pages 118–123

Autobiography

Summary

Author Gary Paulsen recalls duck hunting with his uncle and his dog. Paulsen is nostalgic about much of this childhood experience, including the natural setting. However, his disturbing memory of killing a duck helps explain why he now lives in the "real world" and no longer hunts.

Reading Hint	Thinking Skill	Extension
Point out that even though Paulsen writes about himself in the third person as "the boy," the story is autobiographical.	Ask students to *analyze* why Paulsen did not give up hunting after killing the doe.	**Other Points of Views:** Ask students to write a brief description of killing the duck from the point of view of Paulsen's uncle.

Discussing the Autobiography

1. What unpleasant sensations does the author recall from being in the swamp? (Recall) *Examples include the rainy cold mornings when "nobody sane went outside," the mud that would try to "suck a boot off," and the smell of whiskey and coffee in his uncle's truck.*

2. Why do you think Paulsen feels such longing and affection for the duck hunt that was at times so unpleasant for him? (Analysis) *Answers will vary. Nature, even when unpleasant, rewarded the author with a variety of strong sensations, including a sense of great adventure.*

3. What pleasant sensations does the author recall from being in the swamp? (Recall) *Examples include cuddling with the warm dog in the cold truck, the uncle talking to his dog in a soft, even voice, and the experience of using a fine weapon.*

4. What does the author mean when he says that the onset of "moral doubt" ended his childhood? (Analysis) *Answers will vary. When Paulsen killed the duck, he saw it as "broken." That vision made him worry that he had done the wrong thing. That moment of doubt ended, or "killed," his childhood.*

Special Focus: The Hunting Debate

Humans have hunted animals for food for thousands of years. But in many parts of the world, hunting is no longer a necessity. As Paulsen's autobiography implies, today hunting is often considered a sport that measures skill, provides the thrill of the chase, and offers the benefits of outdoor life. However, unregulated hunting once caused the extinction or near-loss of some species. On the other hand, leaving too many wild creatures in any given habitat can result in their starvation, as well as damage to the environment.

Use questions such as the following to discuss hunting with your students.

- Do you think people have a natural instinct to hunt? Why or why not?
- Do you think that hunting is necessary for the management of game and the environment? Explain your answers.
- Do you think there is an ethical difference between hunting for food and hunting for sport? If so, explain.

The Last Dog   by Katherine Paterson, pages 124–137   Short Story

Summary

A boy of the future finds an orphaned puppy when he ventures outside the highly controlled dome in which the human race now lives. The people have created the dome as a safe haven because of their belief that the earth is irreparably damaged by pollution. When scientists plan experiments on the animal, the boy takes the puppy and abandons the dome and its constrictions for good.

Reading Hint	Thinking Skill	Extension
Help students identify references to "ancient fictions" such as *Huck Finn*, *M.C. Higgins the Great*, *Jo*, *Lassie*, *Toto*, *Sounder*, *Travis Coates*, and *Old Yeller*.	In some ways this story is about the fear of nature. Do you see evidence of such fear in today's society? Explain.	**Virtual Reality:** Have students discuss the drawbacks and benefits of virtual reality. Would they rather take a simulated roller coaster ride or a real one? Attend a virtual school or a real one? Learn a skill such as surgery through real experience or virtual reality?

Vocabulary

copious plentiful; abundant

cull gather; pick out

evasive vague; unspecific

forays invasions; raids

interfacing interacting; connecting

languishing drooping; fading

objectivity fairness; neutrality

provocation prompting; motive

reproof scolding; disapproval

tentatively uncertainly; hesitantly

Discussing the Short Story

1. What has happened to the family unit in Brock's society? (Recall) *Families were done away with because they were considered wasteful. Children are conceived and born in a lab and raised in pods by a bank of computers and a podmaster.*
2. What do the researchers mean when they say that Brock had "become crippled by primal urges"? (Analysis) *They feel he can no longer make sound decisions because he is being influenced by primitive feelings such as love, joy, and pleasure.*
3. Why does Brock leave the security of the dome? (Analysis) *Answers will vary. Brock discovers that life in the dome was stifling.*

He doesn't want to give up his newly discovered feelings or the puppy, so leaving the dome seems worth the risk.

4. What do you think Brock will find outside the dome? (Analysis) *Answers will vary. Some students may suggest that Brock will find a society of "deviants" who, in the past, ventured out of the dome. Others will point out that the puppy's father is probably still alive and that Brock may find it as well, perhaps living with the deviants.*

Special Focus: Outside vs. Inside

The people in this story live inside the controlled environment of a dome because they fear the dangers of the hostile and damaged world outside. In some ways, our real world is like a series of mini-domes, with skywalks over downtown streets and a vast network of interstates that we travel on in cars with our windows rolled up.

Ask students the following questions.

- How is a shopping mall like a dome society?
- How have air conditioning and home entertainment such as television and computer games affected the way people spend leisure time in warm weather?
- Would you rather stroll through a carefully planned botanical garden or a forest undeveloped for recreation?

Is the Weather Getting Worse?

Article

by Colin Marquis and Stu Ostro, pages 138–141

Summary

Two meteorologists suggest that recent severe weather trends may be normal rather than a sign that the weather is getting worse. They give examples of ways that incomplete or biased information can influence people's perceptions.

Reading Hint	Thinking Skill	Extension
Point out that this article identifies some important factors that affect people's perceptions of information.	From their own observations, do students think the weather is getting worse? Why or why not?	**For and Against:** Ask students to find two sets of facts in the article: those that indicate the weather is getting worse and those that indicate it is not.

Vocabulary

albeit although; even if

benign kind; mild

expositions explanations; speeches

induced caused; created

inundated flooded; overwhelmed

ominous threatening; forbidding

uninhibited unstopped; unchecked

versatile clever; able to do many things

vicariously through another; indirectly

Discussing the Article

1. According to this article, what can affect or distort people's perceptions of weather patterns? (Recall) *Major factors include instant media coverage of disasters, the use of satellites to report land and water temperatures, an increase in population, newly crowded and expensive coastal developments, and increased reporting of hurricanes.*

2. How could growth in population potentially affect weather patterns? (Analysis) *Answers will vary. Cutting down trees for more buildings results in less shade and therefore more heat. More concrete and asphalt for roads and parking lots results in more heat and a decrease in the natural water runoff, which causes flooding. As more people crowd into certain areas (especially along the coasts) there are more injuries and expensive damages when a storm hits.*

3. What do meteorologists mean when they say that the weather "pendulum is beginning to swing back—toward the wild side"? (Analysis) *Answers will vary. Meteorologists have discovered that drastic changes in temperature and precipitation took place long before humans could have affected the weather. The writers suggest that these seemingly extreme climate changes are normal and that it may be time for some wilder weather, regardless of human intervention.*

Special Focus: Worst Case Scenarios

A worst case scenario takes the facts about an issue or incident and imagines the worst outcome to which they could lead. In "The Last Dog," for example, a worst case scenario has already occurred: the world is so polluted people believe they cannot live in it.

Trigger a discussion of this concept with the following.

- What other selections in this book deal with worst case scenarios? *Students' answers may include: "And They Lived Happily Ever After for a While," "Is Humanity a Special Threat?", and "A Young Environmentalist Speaks Out."*
- What motivates people to imagine worst case scenarios?
- What are some good and bad results of thinking about worst case scenarios?

The Last Street by Abraham Reisen, page 142

Poem

Summary

The speaker describes a quiet street located where the city ends and the countryside begins.

Reading Hint	Thinking Skill	Extension
Tell students that Reisen lived from 1876 to 1953. Is the poem applicable today?	Ask students to note the poet's use of simple words and phrases. Does the language enhance the message of the poem? Why or why not?	**Writing a Poem:** Tell students that the poet is making a strong contrast between the city and the country. Have students write a poem that does the same thing.

Discussing the Poem

1. What setting is the speaker describing? (Recall) *The speaker is describing the last street in a town, where city meets country.*

2. What contrast does the speaker make between the last street and the city? (Recall) *The speaker points out that the last street is much quieter than the rest of the city because it borders open fields and because the residents live quietly.*

3. Why does the speaker take pleasure in the scene? (Analysis) *Answers will vary. The speaker shows that one's vision is not blocked here and that a person can take in the vista of the fields and the expanse of the sky.*

4. Do you agree with the speaker's lines, "Here where city ends, / The world begins"? (Analysis) *Answers will vary. Students might offer that the speaker implies that life can be lived more meaningfully in the country than the city.*

Special Focus: Noise Pollution

Unwanted sound is called *noise pollution*. For example, people may be bothered by the sounds of airplanes, traffic, or machinery. Research has shown that continuous exposure to very loud noises can cause hearing loss, stress, high blood pressure, anxiety, sleep loss, and an inability to concentrate. Use questions such as the following to discuss the problems of noise pollution with your class.

- Do you consider noise pollution a true type of pollution? Why or why not?
- Do you think an older person's definition of noise pollution differs from a younger person's? Explain.
- What are some steps that can be taken to protect people from typical noises that occur in day-to-day life?
- Some people like silence; others are uncomfortable without background noise. Which do you prefer and why?

Cluster Four Vocabulary Test

Vocabulary Words

Choose the meaning of the bold word in each passage.

1. Coming up here today, I have no hidden **agenda**. *("A Young Environmentalist Speaks Out," p. 111)*

   Ⓐ secret   Ⓒ suspicion
   Ⓑ plan   Ⓓ regret

2. In Europe, Westminster Abbey was **consecrated** . . . *("The Mushroom, p. 114)*

   Ⓐ destroyed   Ⓒ blessed
   Ⓑ abandoned   Ⓓ built

3. The comet was as **indifferent** as the forest and the mushroom to the affairs of human-kind. *("The Mushroom," p. 115)*

   Ⓐ unconcerned   Ⓒ sympathetic
   Ⓑ interested   Ⓓ unmerciful

4. **Inexorably** the settlers came, cutting, burning, blasting, plowing around the stumps. *("The Mushroom," p. 116)*

   Ⓐ tirelessly   Ⓒ unavoidably
   Ⓑ openly   Ⓓ purposely

5. He tried to ask the clerk who outfitted him, but the woman was **evasive**. *("The Last Dog," p. 126)*

   Ⓐ quiet   Ⓒ upset
   Ⓑ vague   Ⓓ not listening

6. The pup licked his glove **tentatively**, then backed away again. *("The Last Dog," pp. 130–131)*

   Ⓐ uncertainly   Ⓒ affectionately
   Ⓑ playfully   Ⓓ hungrily

7. For the first week, the researchers seemed quite content to observe dog and boy from their glass-paneled observation booth and speak **copious** notes into their computers. *("The Last Dog," p. 134)*

   Ⓐ brief   Ⓒ misleading
   Ⓑ abundant   Ⓓ excellent

8. It's as if we're all experiencing the bad weather . . . **vicariously**. *("Is the Weather Getting Worse?" p. 139)*

   Ⓐ in isolation   Ⓒ consciously
   Ⓑ fearfully   Ⓓ through another

9. Extremes will always occur, and they do not necessarily foretell of more **ominous** times to come. *("Is the Weather Getting Worse?" p. 140)*

   Ⓐ threatening   Ⓒ pleasant
   Ⓑ discouraging   Ⓓ bizarre

10. With nearly **uninhibited** [population] growth continuing along the nation's coasts and the inevitability of strong ocean storms, losses will continue to rise. *("Is the Weather Getting Worse?" p. 141)*

    Ⓐ mind-boggling   Ⓒ unstopped
    Ⓑ unreasonable   Ⓓ nonexistent

Research, Writing, and Discussion Topics

The following are suggested topics you might research, write about, or discuss.

1. *Evaluate* media coverage of a particular ecological issue.
2. Find an essay, article, or story that centers on an environmental issue. *Evaluate* whether the piece would be a good addition to this anthology.
3. Read a science fiction novel and *analyze* the author's view of the environment of the future.
4. Discuss what you think the ecological condition of the world will be 25 years from now.
5. *Analyze* the success of a particular campaign aimed at saving the environment.
6. Research an environmental issue and use *problem-solving* skills to devise a plan for solving the problem.
7. Use *problem-solving* skills to decide how to create more interest in environmental issues among the general population.

8. Use *problem-solving* skills to create a booklet of environmental tips for students.
9. Take a survey about an environmental issue. Include questions about how serious people think the problem is and how willing they would be to become involved in solving it. *Synthesize* the results into a chart or report of your findings.
10. Use *synthesis* to create a visual or written product that conveys the seriousness of an environmental issue.
11. *Compare and contrast* two sides of an environmental issue such as global warming or urban sprawl.
12. Discuss environmental concerns in your community, using *problem-solving* skills to consider what you could do individually or as a group to help solve problems.

Assessment and Project Ideas

Extended Research Opportunities

Here are some topics that you may wish to investigate further and report on either in writing or in an oral presentation to the class.

- A particular species that is endangered because of human actions
- American Indian views of nature
- Environmental issues in the news today
- Genetically modified plants
- Medicinally useful plants found in the rain forest
- Cases in which the earth has recovered from environmental damage, either on its own or with human help
- An animal rights group
- Life as a Jain, a vegetarian, an avid recycler, or some other kind of person who works hard to help the environment
- Animals that are killed for "ornamental" purposes
- The origins and history of Earth Day
- Animal research laboratories

Speaking and Listening

1. Debate the following: "Modifying the genetic makeup of plants should be illegal."
2. Deliver a speech on some environmental issue that you would like to present to someone in local, state, or federal government.
3. Present a news report on a particular environmental crisis or on an effective solution to such a crisis.
4. Assume the role of a representative of an industry that has been accused of causing an environmental problem. Deliver a talk presenting the industry's point of view.
5. Debate the following: "Animals are on earth for the use of human beings."

Creative Writing

1. Write a scene for a situation comedy that uses humor to call attention to an environmental issue.
2. Write a science fiction story that describes the environment of the future.
3. Write a story or a scene in script form in which two people have opposite opinions on an environmental issue. Bring their disagreement to some resolution.
4. Review a movie such as "Born Free" or "The China Syndrome" centered on a particular environmental issue.
5. Create a poem or song that reflects your view about an environmental issue.

Artistic Expression

1. Design an ad or poster that calls attention to a particular environmental threat or to an environmentally helpful product or service.
2. Make a painting, drawing, or sculpture that expresses your feelings about some aspect of nature.
3. Take photographs and create a photo essay on an environmental issue in your own area. Alternatively, create realistic illustrations for such an essay.
4. Create a comic book or picture book of a folk tale or other story that draws attention to the natural world.

Essay Test

Using what you have learned while reading *What on Earth?* and what you already know, respond to the prompt below. Note: This is an open-book test. Use quotations and details from the selections to support your response.

Prompt: How do we protect our planet?

General Standards and Criteria for Project Evaluation

Apply those standards that fit the specific project. Some standards might not be used.

Standards	Criteria			
Areas of Assessment	**High**	**Very Good**	**Adequate**	**Needs Work**
Research and Preparation • Resources • Evidence • Deadlines • Use of Time	❑ used a variety of challenging, reliable, and appropriate resources ❑ used appropriate evidence and examples ❑ met all deadlines ❑ used any extra time to extend research	❑ used several reliable, appropriate resources ❑ made effort to use evidence and examples ❑ met deadlines ❑ used preparation time well	❑ used minimum number of resources for basic information ❑ used some evidence and examples ❑ needed encouragement to meet deadlines ❑ spent minimal time on preparation	❑ used few resources ❑ used little evidence and few examples ❑ didn't meet all deadlines ❑ spent little time on preparation
Content • Purpose • Organization • Audience Appeal • Information • Sources	❑ creatively fulfilled purpose ❑ used logical, easy-to-follow order ❑ created and maintained high audience interest ❑ covered topic with outstanding information ❑ credited sources	❑ completely fulfilled purpose ❑ used easy-to-follow order ❑ kept audience's attention ❑ covered topic with appropriate information ❑ credited sources	❑ fulfilled purpose ❑ used order that was confusing at times ❑ lost audience's attention at times ❑ covered the basics ❑ credited sources	❑ did not fulfill purpose ❑ used hard-to-follow order ❑ created little audience interest ❑ omitted important information ❑ provided incomplete credits
Visual Elements • Audience Appeal • Purpose • Effectiveness • Effort	❑ were highly interesting, easy to see and understand ❑ supported purpose ❑ communicated main ideas clearly ❑ showed outstanding effort	❑ were interesting, easy to see and understand ❑ supported purpose ❑ communicated main ideas ❑ showed effort	❑ were somewhat interesting ❑ were related to purpose ❑ generally supported main ideas ❑ showed fair effort	❑ were messy, disorganized, hard to understand ❑ were unrelated to purpose ❑ didn't support main ideas ❑ showed little effort
Written Elements • Accuracy • Revision • Details	❑ had few errors ❑ were thoroughly proofread and revised ❑ supported main ideas with rich details	❑ had few errors ❑ were proofread and revised ❑ supported main ideas	❑ had several errors ❑ needed more proofreading and revision ❑ weakly supported main ideas	❑ had many errors ❑ needed to be proofread and revised ❑ didn't support main ideas
Oral Presentation • Delivery • Props • Eye Contact	❑ spoke audibly and expressively ❑ used engaging gestures and props ❑ maintained excellent eye contact	❑ spoke audibly and expressively ❑ used gestures and props ❑ maintained good eye contact	❑ could develop more expression ❑ used few or awkward gestures and props ❑ attempted to maintain eye contact	❑ was difficult to hear ❑ used few or distracting gestures and props ❑ made little attempt to maintain eye contact

Choose from the following selections to enhance and extend the themes in this *Literature &
Thought* anthology. The letters *RL* in the brackets indicate the reading level of the book listed. *IL*
indicates the approximate interest level. Perfection Learning's catalog numbers are included for
your ordering convenience.

Challenging

Pilgrim at Tinker Creek by Annie Dillard. Personal narrative on ecology and the importance of
nature from the author's one-year exploration of her own neighborhood. Pulitzer Prize winner.
[RL 9 IL 9 +] Paperback 5597301; Cover Craft 5597302.

Average

The Ancient One by T.A. Barron. While exploring the lush Oregon wilderness, 13-year-old Kate
finds herself thrust back in time 500 years. There, she learns the important balance of humans'
relationship with the earth. [RL 7 IL 7 +] Paperback 4622301; Cover Craft 4622302.

Phoenix Rising by Karen Hesse. Thirteen-year-old Nyle learns about relationships and death
when 15-year-old Ezra, who was exposed to radiation leaked from a nearby nuclear plant,
comes to stay at her grandmother's Vermont farmhouse. [RL 6 IL 5–9] Paperback 4805001;
Cover Craft 4805002.

Planet Earth: Egotists & Ecosystems by Roger Rosen & Patra McSharry, eds. An international
look at ecology, from the rain forests of Brazil to the streets of Dublin. Icarus World Issues
Series. [RL 7 IL 9 +] Paperback 4270501; Cover Craft 4270502.

Shadows in the Water by Kathryn Lasky. When Mr. Starbuck accepts a job with the
Environmental Protection Agency, the family moves to a houseboat in the Florida Keys. They
soon discover the fragile ecosystem of the Keys is in danger and set out to stop the culprits.
[RL 6 IL 3–7] Paperback 4483901; Cover Craft 4483902.

The Weirdo by Theodore Taylor. In this environmental thriller, 17-year-old Chip Clewt fights to
save the black bears in the Powhatan National Wildlife Refuge. [RL 6.1 IL 5–10] Paperback
4544601; Cover Craft 4544602.

The Wolfling by Sterling North. In the 19th-century midwest, a young boy adopts a wolf whelp
and gains the attention and friendship of the Swedish-American naturalist, Thure Kumlien.
[RL 6 IL 5–9] Paperback 9270501; Cover Craft 9270502.

Easy

Fighting for Survival by Anne Marshall. Five stories about being on the front line fighting to
protect wildlife and wild places. Topics covered are Chincoteague ponies, alligators, Columbia
River salmon, the American wolf, and big game. Into The Wild Places #1. [RL 5 IL 5 +]
Paperback 5948601; Cover Craft 5948602.

Lostman's River by Cynthia DeFelice. Ty MacCauley comes to grips with his disturbing discovery
that good and evil are not absolutes, and at the same time his parents must decide whether they
will keep hiding or face the future. [RL 5.5 IL 4–8] Paperback 4913901; Cover Craft 4913902.

A Place Called Ugly by Avi. At the end of the summer, 14-year-old Owen refuses to leave the
beach house which has been his family's summer home for 10 years and is scheduled for
demolition. [RL 5.8 IL 5–9] Paperback 4646001; Cover Craft 4646002.

Shadowmaker by Joan Lowery Nixon. After she and her mother move to a small Texas town
and experience a series of menacing events, Katie begins to suspect there is something sinister
going on involving a secret gang of high schoolers and illegally stored toxic waste. [RL 5.9
IL 7 +] Paperback 4795801; Cover Craft 4795802.

The Talking Earth by Jean Craighead George. Billie Wind ventures out alone into the Florida
Everglades to test the legend of her Indian ancestors and learns the importance of listening to
the earth's vital messages. [RL 5 IL 6–10] Paperback 8714001; Cover Craft 8714002.

What Do You Think?

You are about to begin a unit of study on the theme of ecology. Mark the following statements by putting an *A* or *D* on the lines. This is not a test. Think of it as a way to find out what you feel about the themes and issues related to the environment.

Agree or Disagree (Write an *A* or *D* by each statement.)

_____ 1. Eventually humans will have to wear oxygen masks to survive the effects of air pollution.

_____ 2. After either a man-made or natural disaster occurs, the earth is often able to heal itself.

_____ 3. It is the duty of humans to protect wildlife.

_____ 4. Since extinction is a natural process, it doesn't matter if humans cause the extinction of a certain species.

_____ 5. Overpopulation is a crucial problem throughout the world.

_____ 6. Most Americans are not willing to be inconvenienced to help solve an environmental issue.

_____ 7. Hunting is murder and should be banned.

_____ 8. In the last few years, the weather has gotten much worse due to man-made causes.

Vocabulary Test Answers

Cluster One Vocabulary Test

1. C; 2. B; 3. B; 4. B; 5. A; 6. B; 7. D; 8. A; 9. A; 10. A

Cluster Two Vocabulary Test

1. C; 2. A; 3. B; 4. A; 5. D; 6. D; 7. C; 8. D; 9. A; 10. B

Cluster Three Vocabulary Test

1. C; 2. D; 3. B; 4. C; 5. D; 6. D; 7. A; 8. A; 9. A; 10. B

Cluster Four Vocabulary Test

1. B; 2. C; 3. A; 4. C; 5. B; 6. A; 7. B; 8. D; 9. A; 10. C